All about the
St. Bernard

3rd edition

Rachel Beaver

The St Bernard

Behold this creature's form and state
Which nature therefore did create,
That to the world might be expressed
What mien there can be in a beast;
And that we in this shape may find
A lion of another kind.
For this heroic beast does seem
In majesty to rival him,
And yet vouchsafes to man to show
Both service and submission too.
For whence we this distinction have:
That beast is fierce, but that is brave.
This dog have so himself subdued
That hunger cannot make him rude,
And his behaviour does confess
True courage dwells with gentleness.

From ***The St Bernard*** by **Frederick Gresham** (1907)

Cover: Ch Finetime Pilot's Pal, owned by Sq Ldr and Mrs P Flint.
Title page: Ch Whaplode Unique
Contents page: Three Whaplode Champions.
Owned by Mr and Mrs J Harpham.

The whelping illustrations in Chapter 8 are by Angela Begg.

contents

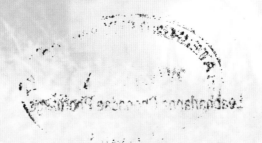

introduction

The St Bernard world has changed greatly since the first edition of this book was published in 1980. In this country, new breeders and exhibitors have sprung into prominence, and some well-known names from the past are sadly no longer with us. Breed type has altered, arguably not always for the better, and The Kennel Club has drastically reduced the number of Challenge Certificates available to St Bernard exhibitors. The Kennel Club Breed Standard has been amended, widening even further the difference between the wording of the standard used in this country and that in force elsewhere in the world. Two great continental experts on the breed, Dr Antonio Morsiani and Albert de la Rie, have passed away. Both were detractors of the English St Bernard. Recent years have seen a surge in the popularity of a type of St Bernard currently being bred in Scandinavia and now exported worldwide.

With the modern trend towards international cooperation in Europe and the possibility of eventual easing of quarantine regulations, it seems inevitable that there will be more interbreeding between European and British dogs. Hopefully, we shall all be able to acknowledge merit, where it exists, in types of Saint other than our own. We must also trust that British St Bernard breeders will always strive to retain the expressive head type, benevolence and impression of power that is still seen today in the cream of our stock.

My husband, Richard Beaver, died in 1991 after a long and brave battle against cancer. He was always a fighter, and never spared his efforts on behalf of the breed he loved. The task of updating this book has fallen to me, and it has not been easy without his knowledge and encouragement. He wrote the introduction to the first edition of the book, and some of the points he made then may still be of interest today. He told how, after World War II, he went to live at Northbourne in Kent, where he kept and worked gundogs. Here he met the late Mrs Graydon Bradley, who kept a large kennel of her Boystown St Bernards at nearby Whitfield Hall. She introduced him to Mrs Harding, of Sholden Grange, who gave him his first St Bernard. This was a bitch out of Boystown Carol by a son of Ch Cornagarth Just Right. A second bitch of the same breeding, known as Gershwin Melody, followed and won two Challenge Certificates (CCs). In those days, the great Cornagarth and Peldartor kennels dominated the show ring, and a breeder was lucky to take home a card of any colour from a Championship Show.

After our marriage, Richard and I began to breed St Bernards under the affix Lindenhall. Our first litter came from a daughter of Gershwin Melody, kindly lent to us by a friend for breeding. This bitch was mated to Ch Cornagarth Carlos and bred us Ch Lindenhall High Hopes, who was Best St Bernard Bitch at Crufts in 1975.

I can well remember how, as a child, I was often taken for a brisk walk on Sunday afternoons. Frequently this went in the direction of Cliffsend Hall, near Pegwell Bay, where the late Mrs Scales had her kennel. Notices outside the great iron gates warned that St Bernard dogs were loose in the grounds, and often a group of the massive creatures would be waiting behind the gates, ready to make friends with all who passed. Richard and I had not been married long when we were asked to give a home to an elderly St Bernard bitch. This proved to be none other than the last of Mrs Scales's dogs, Sally, who had to leave the Hall when it was sold after the death of her mistress. She settled down very happily with us but, when we moved from Kent to Derbyshire, she seemed to sense another disruption in her old life. She never recovered from the move, dying peacefully in her sleep soon afterwards at the age of twelve.

In the past, when families visited our home in search of a puppy, my husband would always point out at great length the disadvantages and responsibilities that St Bernard ownership entailed. It was patiently explained that beauty and benevolence were accompanied by phenomenal strength and voracious appetite, and that the costs involved were proportional to the size of the dog. Visitors were treated to lurid descriptions of muddy footprints on carpets, piles of moulted hair, slavering jaws, mounds of stinking offal, and sonorous snores pervading the house throughout the night. If these warnings prevented placing a puppy in a home where it would eventually become unwelcome, my husband felt that time had been well spent. If, after warnings, prospective owners were still convinced that a St Bernard was the dog for them, it was revealed that, although the romantic legend of the life-saver of the Alps complete with brandy barrel was out of date, the St Bernard, if properly reared and trained, was indeed the King of Dogs, as its rôle as the emblem of Crufts Show implied; that this breed possessed all the good qualities to be looked for in a dog, being faithful, loving, intelligent and gentle, and making numerous friends wherever it took its owner.

It is still true today that new St Bernard owners become, as it were, members of a race apart, and their living habits are gently but inexorably changed. Larger cars, frequently of the estate type, appear in their driveways; low tables vanish from living rooms; bolts are placed on easily-opened doors; and gardens, if small, cease to be places of beauty and become mud patches. In addition to this, strange carvings and models of St Bernards appear on the mantlepiece and brandy barrels that have never held a drop of the hard stuff are seen strangely suspended from walls.

I am very grateful to TFH/Kingdom Books for giving me the opportunity to prepare this new edition of *All About the St Bernard*. I should like to thank everyone who has supplied modern photographs and new information. Some of those approached must have thought me a great nuisance when I pestered them for material. If the book helps in any way to further the knowledge, progress and well-being of the breed, I hope they will feel that their trouble has been worthwhile.

Rachel Beaver
Old Tupton, Derbyshire

Chapter One

The St Bernard Hospice and its Dogs

The Hospice of the Great St Bernard stands at over 2440m (8000ft) above sea level at the top of the Great St Bernard Pass in the Swiss Canton of Valais. It is one of the highest human habitations in Europe. Lacking the beauty of many other mountain passes, the Great St Bernard is a place of bleak snow-covered rocks and jagged peaks, which tower over the Hospice buildings huddled beneath them. On the Plan de Jupiter, a small plateau formerly occupied by the Temple of Jupiter, stands the iron statue of St Bernard pointing the way to his Hospice.

'You who climb the Alps in safety under my guidance,' says the plaque below, 'continue with me into the House of Heaven.'

The climate in the pass is such that little vegetation can grow, and a few pine trees about 610m (2000ft) below are the only signs of life on the treacherous slopes. The temperature rises above freezing point for only about 20 days each year, and the small lake in front of the buildings, which forms part of the boundary between Italy and Switzerland, is sometimes frozen throughout the year. During the winter months, the snow has been known to reach a depth of 11m (36ft) around the buildings, and it is possible to ski right out of the windows on the second storey.

Until the construction of the St Bernard Tunnel, this pass on the main road between Italy and Northern Europe was one of the most important routes across the Alps. The Romans improved it during the first century AD, and it was much used by Christian pilgrims travelling to the Tomb of the Apostles in Rome. These people were often attacked by gangs of Saracen robbers, who lay in wait for travellers, using as their main hide-out the ruins of the Mons Jovis temple.

Bernard de Menthon was born in Savoy at the end of the 10th century AD. He was the son of Richard de Menthon, a wealthy baron who resided at the Castle of Menthon on the Lake of Annecy. Bernard studied theology in Paris until his proud parents demanded his return to Menthon to marry a rich heiress. Determined to become a monk, he tore the bars from his window and escaped on the night before the wedding. He fled to the Augustinian Cathedral at Aosta in Italy, where he later became a canon, and eventually Archdeacon.

According to legend, frightened villagers burst in one night as Bernard was praying in his chapel. They claimed to have been attacked by the demon, Procus, who was said to be at the Mons Jovis temple. Bernard led the villagers through a terrible storm to the temple, where Procus turned himself into a dragon. Bernard threw his stole around the demon's neck and it turned into a chain, which held him down while Bernard slew him. The villagers demolished the statue of Jupiter, and Bernard told them to build a Hospice in the pass for the shelter and protection of travellers. This they did in about 962 AD, dragging some of the stone for many miles over icy tracks and constructing a simple building like one of the refuge huts often found in the mountains. Bernard's parents, who had been grief-stricken since his departure, visited him there, and donated much of their wealth towards the completion and maintenance of his Hospice. Before his death at the age of 85 he is said to have founded 160 monasteries and convents and served as an Archdeacon for 40 years.

The ancestry of the dogs

It is impossible to say accurately when dogs were first introduced to the Hospice, as all its early archives were destroyed in a disastrous fire in 1555. A picture of St Bernard in the Hospice today shows him with a dog, but this was given to the monks in 1870 by a Parisian gentleman and is of 19th century origin.

It is likely that dogs were first taken to the Hospice between 1660 and 1670. They would have been of a local herd-dog type, obtained from the surrounding valleys. The

The St Bernard Hospice in winter.

origin of these Swiss mountain dogs, and so also of the St Bernard, has been a matter of surmise for many years, and various theories have been put forward.

All the members of the Mastiff group, to which the St Bernard belongs, are of heavy weight and bone, with large square heads, well-defined stops, and short square muzzles. Since no traces of dogs of this type have yet been found amongst the prehistoric remains of Europe, we must look further afield for the ancestors of the St Bernard. Our search takes us to ancient Tibet where, in a breed known as the Tibetan Mastiff, lies the most probable answer to our question.

Tibetan Mastiffs were used as monastery guards and regarded as a holy breed, so they survived unchanged over the centuries. They were and are of great size and weight, with strong heads, heavily-boned legs and five-toed feet. In the Middle Ages, Marco Polo wrote: *The people of Tibet possess a large number of powerful and excellent dogs, which render great service at the capture of musk deer. They keep dogs as big as donkeys, which are excellent for hunting wild animals, especially yak.*

According to ancient writers, these large dogs from Tibet were acquired by other races and eventually introduced to Assyria and Babylon. Assyrian bas reliefs of hunting scenes in the British Museum show dogs strongly resembling the modern St Bernard. The Assyrians also used them as war dogs and introduced them to Egypt. In 470 BC, Xerxes, King of Persia, is believed to have taken some to Greece, but it was Alexander the Great who finally established them in Europe. On his march to the Indus, he is said to have received many presents of enormous dogs, trained to do battle with lions and elephants. His tutor, Aristotle, gave them the name *Leontonix*, meaning sons of lions, as it was believed that these dogs had originally arisen from a cross between a dog and a lion. Though this would seem biologically impossible, St Bernards often resemble great cats in attitude and expression.

One of Alexander's heirs, Pyrrhus, King of Epirus, temporarily conquered Italy, so the dogs were introduced to the Romans. They called the breed Canis Molossus, after the town of Molossis in Epirus where they believed the dogs had originated. The dogs battled in the arenas of Rome and were used for guard and herding duties.

The Roman Molossus dog developed into two distinct types. One, of slighter build and light colour and with a long head, was used as a herding dog; the other, heavier, more massive, dark-coated and broad-headed, was used for guard duties and as a fighting dog. The St Bernard and the Mastiff are almost certainly descended from this heavier type of Molossus. The name Mastiff may well be a derivation of the Latin word *massivus*.

As the Roman armies advanced northwards into Europe over the Alps their dogs accompanied them. In about 40 BC the Roman invaders travelled across the St Bernard pass into Switzerland and built their temple to Jupiter. At this time, the lighter type of herding Molossus was introduced into the valleys. Today it is represented by the small type of Swiss herd dog known as the Sennenhunde, of which there are several varieties, including the Bernese Mountain Dog. During later Roman invasions in the first and second centuries AD, the heavier type of Molossus reached Switzerland. These dogs remained as guards in the passes, and in the Aosta and Valais districts, the eventual home of the St Bernard. Later they were used not only as guards but also as working farm dogs. They are believed to have developed into the larger breeds of herd dog.

Throughout the centuries the Valais district remained geographically isolated because of the few routes of

The statue of St Bernard de Menthon and the 'Pain de Sucre' (2900m or 9517 ft) high.

communication with other areas. A pure strain of dogs therefore developed there, as only occasionally was foreign blood introduced. In the 17th century when the Hospice monks began to use dogs in Alpine rescue, they naturally used dogs of the pure Valais strain for their original stock. The world-wide fame so worthily earned by the rescue dogs at the Hospice led eventually to the breed name St Bernard, but one should remember that this unique type of dog developed initially not only at the Hospice but in the whole Valais district.

The monks and their dogs

The earliest reference to dogs in the Hospice archives is in 1774 when it is stated that a dog was killed by an avalanche. In the following year there is mention of a Canon Cosmos making a wheel in which a dog is placed to turn the spit. With hundreds of hungry travellers to be fed at all hours of the day and night, meat was constantly roasting on a revolving spit. The monks must have found dogs very useful but, if St Bernards were used, the wheels must have been gigantic!

Writing in 1774, a Swiss author, Bourrit, gives the first clue to the type of dogs used at the Hospice, which he describes as being of extraordinary size, who were trained to help travellers by going in front of them and acting as guides in the midst of cloud and snow. It is clear that, by this date, a new strain of dog had been introduced, whose great size distinguished it from the dogs of the surrounding area, and invited comment. Two Swiss naturalists, writing in 1809, state that the breed then used at the Hospice was that of

A modern statue of St Bernard shows the Saint triumphing over evil.

the Great Dane (Danische Dogge). It was said that a Neapolitan Count, Mazzini, brought back the original dam from his northern travels and presented her to the Hospice on his way across the Great St Bernard. It is probable that the Canons crossed her with their own dogs of the Valais type, so producing the great size that so impressed Bourrit and other writers of the period. By selective breeding the monks developed the distinctive marking of their ideal St Bernard, said to represent the stole, chasuble and scapular of their vestments.

The qualities that make St Bernards so invaluable for Alpine rescue work are well known. St Bernards can scent a human being, against the wind, up to two miles away and locate a body buried by as much as 3.5m of snow. They have a wonderful presentiment that enables them to sense a blizzard about 20 minutes before it occurs. They have been known to give warning of avalanches, standing still and changing course before the dreaded falls take place. All these qualities, together with their great strength, gentleness and ability to work for hours in sub-zero temperatures, have made possible their amazing record of success in Alpine rescue work.

Tibetan Mastiffs – ancestors of the St Bernard.

The most famous of the Hospice dogs was Barry, who worked from 1800 to 1812 and is reputed to have saved at least 40 lives. At the earliest sign of fog or snow, Barry would become restless and demand to be let out. Once outside, he would begin searching in the most remote and dangerous places. Whenever he was unable to dig a person out of the snow himself, he would run back to the Hospice to fetch the monks. There is a story that Barry found a soldier lying in the snow, and that the man, frozen and confused, mistook the dog for a wolf and killed him with his sword. However, it is more probable that, when Barry grew too old for work, the Prior sent him to end his days in retirement with friends at Berne, where he died some two years later. His stuffed body can still be seen there in the Natural History Museum. By tradition, one of the dogs at the Hospice always bore the name Barry after his famous predecessor.

A dramatic tale of a robbery attempt at the Hospice is told by W F Barazetti, author of *The St Bernard Book* and a prominent breeder and exhibitor in Great Britain during the 1950s. It seems that, in October 1787, the monks gave hospitality to two men who arrived at the monastery from Italy. They posed as silversmiths and showed professional interest in the treasures of the Order. The Prior proudly showed them all the valuables, including the 10th-century jewelled crucifix, the heavy golden chalice presented in 1507, and the magnificent collection of Roman coins. The strangers left next morning and retraced their steps to Italy to report what they had seen to the rest of their gang and complete arrangements for a robbery. They planned to take with them a bitch in season to distract the Hospice dogs.

Several days later, when the pass was blanketed in thick dangerous fog, all the dogs left the Hospice with most of the monks to search for lost travellers. Suddenly, one of the dogs stopped dead in his tracks and sniffed the air in the direction of the Hospice. Slowly, he moved again in a strange, uneasy manner, crouching and growling. Then the whole pack made off, rushing madly towards home, the monks running vainly behind them. The monks stumbled and fell, and soon there was no sign of the dogs in the enveloping fog. When they eventually reached the Hospice, the monks found the great door battered open and a scene of silent confusion within. At last the Prior appeared with his robes torn. He told how, soon after he had gone to bed, the Italian gang had arrived and had smashed their way into the building. When he had confronted them, he was forced at pistol point to the chapel to unlock the strong-room containing the treasures. With the two 'silversmiths' guiding them, the gang had loaded the valuables into a leather sack.

Just as they had finished their work, the bitch they had brought with them growled, screamed and fled. There were the Hospice dogs! One made

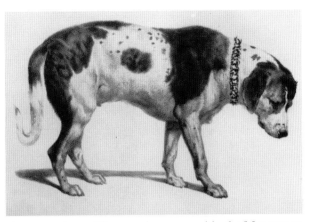

An engraving of Barry as he appeared in the Museum at Berne before his skin was repaired and reset in 1923.

Barry today. Photo: M Heath

straight for the man with the sack, which fell, spilling its contents on the ground. A knife flashed and the dog collapsed, blood spilling over golden coins. In the resultant chaos, the robbers rushed off into the darkness and fog, followed by the enraged pack of dogs. Then there was silence. At midnight, the dogs returned alone, many wounded; of the gang who had tried to rob the Hospice, nothing was ever seen again.

Napoleon reaches the Hospice, 1800.

The story is told of another band of robbers who posed as pilgrims. Having eaten well, they ordered the Prior to take them to the place where the valuables were kept. This Prior, however, was less gullible. He took them to the dogs instead. They left at once – quietly.

Throughout the centuries the Hospice has provided shelter for rich and poor alike. On one occasion, in 1794, 50,000 French émigrés fleeing from the Revolution crossed over the pass. When Napoleon travelled the route in the spring of 1800 on the way to his great victory over the Austrians at Marengo, he was accompanied by an army of 40,000 men and 5000 horses. Each of his 58 cannons was encased in a hollowed-out tree trunk to be dragged up the mountains by a team of 20 grenadiers. When they reached the Hospice, all the soldiers were given hospitality. One of the officers, Captain Coiget wrote: *After fantastic exertions we reached the Hospice. We left the guns and entered. The monks have dedicated a lifetime to the welfare of humanity, helping and refreshing all travellers. The dogs are always at hand to guide those unlucky ones who lose their way, and lead them back to the house where they find help and charity. While our officers and the colonel sat in the hall by the fire, the venerable clergymen gave each twelve men a bucketful of wine, a quarter of cheese, and a pound of bread, and showed us where to rest in those wide passages... We shook hands with the good padres when we left, and we stroked their dogs, who came to us as if they had known us for a long time.*

Napoleon's general, Chambarlhac, who was in charge of the expedition, had to watch helplessly as one gun fell down a precipice, taking 10 soldiers with it before they could free

General Desaix's monument.

their frozen hands from the ropes. When he reached the Hospice, he found he had lost a hundred men. Soon, Napoleon himself arrived, mounted on a mule, and was received by Louis Antoine Luger, the Prior, and two monks.

'Are you three up here on your own all winter?' he asked.

'No, we are about 20 altogether, with our dogs to help us rescue the lost.'

'And where are your men and your dogs while my soldiers perish, may I ask?'

'They are out to rescue them, Sire!'

And so they were. The 10 soldiers who went over the precipice had given up all hope of rescue and, icy and numb, began to drowse in the snow, awaiting a peaceful death. Suddenly, the bark of a dog roused one, who managed to awaken two of his companions. Together they stumbled in the direction of the sound. After a few moments, St Bernards rushed through the snow, followed closely by two monks, and they all turned back to arouse the other seven soldiers and free them from the snow. When the party arrived back at the Hospice, Napoleon was still there. He asked for a personal report and was able to see the dogs. His young general, Desaix, played with the dogs and said they made him feel at home.

Only a fortnight later Napoleon won the victory that was to make him master of Europe for more than a decade, but his favourite, Desaix, lost his life in the battle. Remembering the happy episode at the Hospice, Napoleon ordered that his general's body should be taken there.

The Hospice chapel. Photo: Tony Reed.

'Lay him in the home he chose,' said Napoleon. 'The dogs will guard him well!'

So today the name of General Desaix can still be seen inscribed on a marble plate in the chapel at the Hospice, where his body lies.

Another famous visitor to the Hospice was Queen Victoria, who stayed there one night and later presented the monks with her portrait. During the 1840s she had a dog and a bitch sent to her from Switzerland. Her son, Edward VII, visited the monastery when he was 18, and was presented with a St Bernard puppy, which unfortunately died during the journey home. As a mark of gratitude for the hospitality he had received, he sent the monks a piano and, many years

The Hospice in 1900 (top) and now.

later, after he became king, he sent
another, to show that he had not forgotten
them.

Not all visitors to the Hospice are
human. Twice a year, in April and
October, the monks open the Hospice
windows to admit tens of thousands of
swallows, who enter the buildings to seek
a night's shelter during their long
migratory journey between Europe and
Africa. Also found in the neighbourhood
of the convent are specimens of a singular
sort of ptarmigan, called Herbene. In
winter this bird is completely white; in
spring and summer, black and white
mixed; and in autumn, nearly black.

As the years passed the monks must
constantly have found it necessary to
strengthen their strain by the introduction

Above: A Hospice bitch and her litter, 1994. Top: Dogs at the Hospice, 1960.

of new blood from outside their own kennel. Frequently they outcrossed to dogs in the surrounding Valais region, or used strains from the Simplon or Petit St Bernard Hospices. On neighbouring estates also there were dogs of similar bloodlines. Between 1815 and 1825 all the Hospice dogs are believed to have been destroyed, either by distemper or by an avalanche. Only one bitch remained and she was crossed with a Newfoundland dog. It is said that this mating was the beginning of the rough variety of St Bernard and also increased darkness of coat-colour. However, there had been rough coats as early as 1800, which owed their origin to the rougher type of Sennenhund cross.

Unfortunately, rough coats proved disadvantageous for Alpine rescue as ice-balls formed in the coats, encasing the dogs in frozen strait-jackets. Any rough-coated puppies were either sold or given away to friends nearby, so a distinctive rough type of dog became fairly common in the valleys near the monastery.

The 'St Bernard Express'. Photo: M Heath.

At one time about 20,000 people would cross the Great St Bernard pass each year, many being Italian workmen who went north in the spring in search of work and returned to Italy in late autumn. The road built in 1890 was only passable during the summer months, and was so narrow that up-going traffic was restricted to the morning hours, and downward traffic to the afternoons. Supplies of food, including horsemeat and meal for the dogs, were taken up by road in summer and stored for winter use. Deep freezers were not required.

Between 1888 and 1939 Theophilus Bourgeois was Prior – one of the longest-serving Priors at the Hospice. During this time he did much to improve the conditions at the Hospice. He installed the telephone, electricity and central heating, and also ordered the construction of the building now used as an hotel. With the creation of the Great St Bernard tunnel in 1964 the need for a rescue service has declined considerably, but the number of skiers increases each year.

The dogs are now mainly a tourist attraction. Most of them are taken in winter to warmer accommodation in the valley, and helicopters assist should rescue be necessary. In summer,

Heinrich Schumacher (1831–1903).

noisy hoards of tourists arrive by coach to visit the monastery and view the dogs, now housed behind glass partitions in new kennels. Gift stalls abound, selling St Bernard carvings, models, and stuffed toys at inflated prices. Brandy barrels are sold in their thousands, and some Saints at the Hospice wear them round their necks to amuse the tourists. (The rescue Saints never carried such objects round their necks, although the monks did bring supplies of stimulants to arouse victims lost in the snow.) Barrel-making in Switzerland is another form of big business.

It is sad that the great life-saving breed of the past has been reduced solely to a commercial enterprise.

From rescue dog to show dog

Today's commercialisation of St Bernards at the Hospice and elsewhere echoes events which took place 150 years ago when the breed had a sudden surge in popularity.

The monks had created the St Bernard as a working dog, capable of carrying out its duties under arduous conditions, and they had been highly selective in their breeding programme. They needed strong, smooth-coated dogs of benign, intelligent temperament, and there was no place for passengers in their kennels. Any animals falling short of their exacting standards were passed on to outsiders, who often used them for breeding. Dogs of Hospice type became fairly common in the locality of the monastery. Many were crossed with other breeds, resulting in further variation of type, and any large dog with a modicum of monastery blood in its veins might be sold by the unscrupulous as a Hospice dog.

By the middle of the 19th century, industrial progress had begun to bring more prosperity to certain sections of the community, so it became common practice to keep dogs for pleasure as well as for work. Improvement in road and rail communications made travelling easier, and breeders found it possible to go further afield to acquire better stock and attend shows. The fame of the giant dogs of St Bernard spread further afield, resulting in demand for breeding and show stock from Switzerland.

The first dog show in Britain (confined to Spaniels) was held at the Zoological Gardens, London, in 1843. The first St Bernards were exhibited at Cremorne in 1863, and the sensation created by their appearance led to a craze for the breed in this country. Many of the early imports were of poor quality, but it was mainly from the stock imported from Heinrich Schumacher, of Hollingen, near Berne, that the foundations of the breed in this country were laid. Schumacher (1831–1903), whose picture appears on page 17, made the study of St Bernards his life's work. He was the first fancier outside the Hospice to breed scientifically for his desired type, and he compiled the breed's first stud register. He was said to know every dog of Hospice descent in Switzerland, and his many writings included a detailed history of the breed, issued by the Swiss Kynological Society in 1884. Strangely, he was not a signatory to the Swiss Kynological Society Breed Standard, drawn up in June 1886. However, he published his own opinions in August of that year: *Contribution to the Knowledge of the so-called Great St Bernard Hospice Breed of Dog... compiled from the Traditions of the Monks of the Hospice, and recollections of Heinrich Schumacher.* In this paper Schumacher summarised the state of the breed at that time, and praised the English for the improvements they had made to its development.

The deterioration in the St Bernard breed of dogs is not only the result of deficiency of kynological skill, and of the difficulty in bringing up the very delicate puppies, but also from financial causes. The majority of owners have made the breeding of these noble animals a trade, and, for this reason, consider only their own profit. Moreover, foreign buyers desire long-haired animals, so breeders cross original breeds with long-haired animals, without making the right choice, only to meet the demand.

I do not want to assert that the long-haired St Bernards have depreciated or are less noble, but only that, through faulty or undesirable crossings, and the want of knowledge, depreciation has been facilitated. The long-haired St Bernards are, owing to their mass of hair, larger, more imposing, and more handsome than the short haired (for the long hair can easily cover various shortcomings). The short-haired have the advantage of less perspiration and less

The myth of the St Bernard: the Hospice dogs never wore barrels filled with brandy.

covering for vermin, and are more hardy in various climes.

Englishmen have drawn their St Bernards from Switzerland, and mostly from well-known breeders, and have not, as the Germans erroneously assert, manufactured the St Bernard breed. To the English belong the merit and honour of first recognising and preferring this breed, and of ennobling it, especially by new blood, by which they have contributed very much to the improvement of the whole race.

Schumacher's ideal St Bernard was of the old Barry type, which had been typical of the Hospice dogs before the Newfoundland cross. He favoured a smooth-coated dog of moderate size, and wanted his stock to be able to move like horses, not cattle. He said they had to be active, intelligent and of sound temperament, criticising other Swiss breeders for producing over-large animals with enormous heads and short noses. His breeding stock was acquired from all over the country, including the Hospice, and he sold some of his dogs back to the monks, to improve their own strain. When he brought one pair of dogs to the Hospice in 1866, tears are said to have filled the eyes of the Prior, who said of one of them: 'That is indeed old Barry of 1814 standing there!'

Chapter Two

Early British St Bernards

The first recorded importation of a St Bernard to Britain took place in 1815 when Lion was brought into the country by a Waterloo veteran, together with a bitch. They came into the possession of Mrs Broode of Leasowe Castle, on the Wirral, and several litters were bred from them. Sir Edwin Landseer made a drawing of Lion, which his brother, Thomas, engraved under the title *An Alpine Mastiff*. This name remained in use until about 1850.

'The Leasowe Castle Dog, Lion, 1815'. (After Sir E Landseer)

Lion appears to have been a smooth, short-faced dog, with a good stop, domed skull, diamond eyes and well-arched, compact feet. He was self-coloured except for a short, white blaze. One of his sons, Caesar, is believed to be the standing dog on the right of Landseer's picture *Alpine Mastiffs Re-animating a Traveller*. The other, a bitch, was the property of a Mr T Christmas of Willesden. In 1824, Landseer painted *The Angler's Guard*. The dog in this picture was described as a Newfoundland, but appears to be a typical St Bernard.

Two Smooth Alpine Mastiffs came to Kirklees Hall in Yorkshire in 1825 and were used to build up John Crabtree's famous strain of Mastiffs. The following year, the Rev Ellacombe

'Alpine Mastiffs' (from the painting by Sir E Landseer).

bought a brace of pups from St Remy on the Italian side of the pass. One was kept at Bilton Vicarage, near Bristol, until her death at the age of 17.

In 1831 Mr Dawson of Peckham imported three fawn puppies from the Hospice, and Lord Dashwood purchased several Saints four or five years later, including two from the Grimsel Hospice. At about the same time, Sir Thomas Dick Lauder of North Berwick owned a white dog with orange head markings, said to have been purchased as a puppy from the Hospice.

In the early 1840s Queen Victoria and Prince Albert owned a Smooth dog, Alp, and a Rough bitch, Glory. Where the Royals led others followed, creating an ever-increasing demand for the breed. The Duke of Devonshire had a fine specimen at Chatsworth and, not to be outdone, Lord Harrington owned one at nearby Elvaston Castle.

In 1853 Mr Albert Smith, a well-known expert on Alpine Natural History, imported two Smooth St Bernards from Italy, together with a pair of chamois. They were exhibited the following year at the Egyptian Hall in London, and caused great interest. By this time the old names Alpine Mastiff and Alpine Spaniel had fallen into disuse, and Stonehenge, writing in 1859, refers to The Mount St Bernard Dog, a name which lasted until the mid-1860s.

The first St Bernards to be exhibited in this country were placed first and third in a class for Non-sporting Foreign Dogs (Large) at Birmingham in 1862. They were the property of Mr J Marshall and Mr W Halle, and had no names. The following year, classes were provided for Mount St Bernards at Cremorne and the Agricultural Hall. The two dogs exhibited, both called Monk, were the property of Rev A N Bate and Mr W H Stone. They had no pedigrees but were said to be Hospice bred. Barry, a son of Mr Stone's Monk, won at Cremorne the following year.

Albert Smith's St Bernards and chamois in 1853.

The Rev Cumming MacDona with Tell, c 1868.

At this point the Rev J Cumming MacDona, MP honoured the St Bernard breed with his attentions. He is always regarded as the father of the breed in this country. MacDona was the vicar of Cheadle in Cheshire, but appears to have been a wealthy absentee incumbent. His kennels at Hillbrae House, West Kirby, Wirral housed a number of breeds, including Pointers, Setters, Fox Terriers and Pugs. It was not an uncommon sight to see about 20 of his great St Bernards romping in the sea at West Kirby. He was a member of The Kennel Club Committee and, as such, was entitled to attend shows wearing a silver cross on a crimson ribbon round his neck. There was a class for the breed in 1866 at the National Show in Birmingham, and MacDona won first and second with his Swiss imports, Tell and Bernard.

MacDona made up his mind to establish the best kennel possible and, with this object, paid several visits to Switzerland. He was the first St Bernard fancier in this country to exhibit stock of his own breeding. Tell was a rough-coated, red-brindle and white dog purchased from a breeder in Berne. He had a white chest and legs and black head shading. He would be regarded today as small, and plain in head. He stood 77cm (30.5in) at shoulder and weighed about 68kg (150lb). He was never beaten in the ring in this country. He sired many puppies and was the ancestor of the well-known Save strain. One of his sons, Hope, was presented to the Princess of Wales, later Queen Alexandra. Tell also once saved a child from drowning in the River Dee.

When this famous dog died, MacDona and his wife built a tower near the seashore in his memory. A carving of Tell and a headstone are set into the base of the tower, and a photograph exists showing Mrs MacDona seated beside the grotto, indicating that she, too, was devoted to Tell. The tower and weathered carving still stand today, but now in the garden of one of the dwellings built when Hillbrae House land was sold off in 1980. A spiral staircase has been fitted to the outside, so that one can climb to the ramparts and admire the beautiful views across the estuary of the Dee.

Tell, owned by the Rev Cumming MacDona.

Another St Bernard breeder of importance at this period was Mr J H Murchison, a prominent exhibitor of Fox Terriers and another member of The Kennel Club Committee. From Schumacher's kennels he imported the rough-coated dog Thor, who was much used at stud, although he was said to fail in head. From MacDona, Murchison purchased Monarque, another of Schumacher's breeding.

In 1870, Sir Charles Isham, of Lamport Hall in Northamptonshire, imported a large, rough-coated dog known as Leo, who was white with brindle markings. He was mated to Mr Gresham's Bernie, a daughter of MacDona's Bernard, and had a far-reaching influence on the breed. In an article in *The New Book of the Dog*, Gresham gives an entertaining account of the union and its aftermath:

Bernie was allowed to run about at her own sweet will, until she was three years old, when it occurred to me that, as St Bernards were then becoming popular, I might turn her to good account. But how to make a start was the question, and where to find a sire not too far from home. Leo was the property of Sir Charles Isham, and matters were arranged by the intervention of friends, and the remuneration of a guinea, to be presented to an Orphan Asylum.

In due course a family of 14 arrived, Bernie having selected a standing in a stable for her nursery. The whelps seemed to be of all colours, one a white, another a black. Ignorant of the correct colour of St Bernards, I consulted my groom and was relieved of my anxiety when I heard that the white puppy was somewhat like Leo. The order was, pick out the six biggest and put the other eight into a bucket – they cannot all be kept! Fortunately the black, and also the white puppy were amongst the six biggest. The former lived to be the rough-coated Champion Monk, and the latter Champion Abbess, who was smooth-coated.

Another guinea's worth from Bernie produced a litter of 17, making 31 puppies in less than 12 months. The bucket was not brought into requisition this time.

Abbess, a smooth-coated bitch standing 77cm (30.5in) at shoulder and weighing 68kg (150lb), had many offspring and exerted a considerable influence on the breed. In 1875, her mating to Molke, a son of MacDona's Tell, gave rise to the Save strain from which came numerous winners. Her mating to Murchison's Thor, imported from Schumacher, produced Champions Hector, The Shah, Dagmar, and Abbess II, all in one litter. The following extract from a show catalogue shows the great interest in the breed at this time, and the high prices being asked by breeders.

Sir Charles Isham's Leo.

Abbess, painted by C Burton Barber.

Extract from Catalogue of Grand National Exhibition, held at the Crystal Palace in June 1873

ST BERNARDS (ROUGH & SMOOTH COATED) FOR DOGS ONLY
Champion Classes (for previous winners of Three First Prizes at any Shows)

CLASS 9 ROUGH-COATED
PRIZE: a piece of plate, valued £8.0.0.

94   Mr David Elphinstone Seton   MENTHON   Age 5 years 11 months
Imported from Switzerland.
Not for sale.

95   J H Murchison Esq,   FRGSALP   Age 5 years
Breeder: Rev J C MacDona.
By Gessler-Hedwig. Not for sale.

CLASS 10 SMOOTH-COATED
PRIZE: a piece of plate, value £8.0.0.

96   J H Murchison Esq,   FRGSMONARQUE Age 6 years 3 months
Breeder: H Schumacher. By Souldon. Not for sale.

CLASS 11 ST BERNARDS (ROUGH-COATED) DOGS & BITCHES
First PRIZE: a piece of plate, value £8.0.0.
Second PRIZE: a piece of plate, value £4.0.0.

97	Jose Merino Ballesteros, KGCTC,	FSAURSA	Age 2 years
98	Mr David Elphinstone Seton Not for sale	FRANCE	Age 5 years
99	Mr David Elphinstone Seton Not for sale	TIRASSE	Age 1 year 7 months
100	Mr George James Playfair Price 14 guineas	BARRIS	Age 2 years 3 months
101	Mr James Porter Imported. Not for sale.	VIC	Age 2 years 8 months
102	Miss Hales Imported. Not for sale.	JURA	Age 3 years 6 months
103	Mr William Alfred Joyce Imported. Not for sale.	BERRY	Age 4 years 4 months
104	Mr William Alfred Joyce By Sir Charles Isham's Leo Adam by Mr Stone's Barry. Not for sale.	QUEEN BERTHA	Age 1 year 11 months
105	Mr Richard Simmons Price £210	MACKNEY	Age 2 years 6 months
106	Mr Andrew Pears By Mr Bradshaw's Barry Norma By Mr Sydney's Leo Mount Tell Juno Price 21 guineas	BARRY	Age 19 months
107	Mr C Ellerby Imported. Price £25	WALLACE	Age 11 months
108	Mr William Wilberforce Baynes Breeder: Mr Cochat. Price £250	TURC	Age 2 years last August
109	Mr Elise Marquardt Not for sale	ROLAND	Age 3 years
110	Major Robert S Rous Breeder: Mr Best. Price £200	SAXON	Age 2 years 8 months
111	J H Murchison Esq Breeder: Rev F C Hope-Grant. By HRH The Prince of Wales's Hope-Hedwig. Not for sale.	FRGS MENTOR	Age 11 months 3 days

CLASS 12 ST BERNARDS (SMOOTH-COATED) DOGS & BITCHES

First PRIZE: a piece of plate, value £8.0.0.
Second PRIZE: a piece of plate, value £4.0.0.

112	Mr Percy G Young Imported. Not for sale.	CARLO	Age 2 years 1 month
113	Mr James Clarke	BURNIE	Age 1 year 9 months
114	Mr Fred Gresham Breeder: Exhibitor. By Sir Chas. Isham's Leo – Bernie. Price 11 guineas	BRUCE	Age 2 years 1 month
115	Mr Fred Gresham Breeder: T J Hooper, Esq.	BELLA	Age 2 years 6 months

By Mr Hooper's Barry. Price 11 guineas

117	Miss Aglionby	JURA	Age 2 years 11 months

Bred by the monks of St Bernard.
Price £200

118	Mr James Churton	TIGER	Age 2 years 3 months

Breeder: Mr James McLauglin.
By Pluto – Mona, both imported. Price £60

119	Mr Augustus Smith	MONK	Age 2 years 3 months

Bred by the monks of St Bernard.
Not for sale.

120	Mr George Swan Nottage	BARRY	Age 3 years

Bred at the Monastery of St Bernard.
Not for sale.

121	Mr Henry Wilson Price	CAESAR	Age 2 years 8 months
122	J M Murchison Esq,	FRGS	Age 10 months

Breeder: Exhibitor.   CONSTANCE
By Vansittart's dog ex-owner's Jura.

123	J H Murchison Esq,	FRGS JURA	Age 3 Years

Breeder: Rev J C MacDona.
By Monarque Jungfrau. Not for sale.

124	Mr George Forbes	DRAGON	Age 2 years 10 months

Bred by the monks of the
Hospice of the Great St Bernard.
Not for sale.

125	Rev J C MacDona	MADCHEN	Age 1 year 9 months

Bred by the monks of
St Bernard. Winner of
the 1st Prize and extra
in six classes at Henley,
and second at Glasgow 1873,
the only times exhibited.
Price £1000. In pup to Oscar,
by Monarque – Jungfrau.

Murchison won the first three classes, and MacDona's Madchen triumphed in the final class. The judge was a fellow parson, Rev T Pearce of Morden Vicarage, Blandford, who must have been the counterpart of today's all-rounder. He judged the same breeds at the same show two years later. Judges wore silver crosses with violet ribbons.

In those days, it cost just one guinea (£1.05) to exhibit three dogs, two guineas (£2.10) for six, and so on. There was an additional entry fee of seven shillings and sixpence (37$\frac{1}{2}$p) for each large dog. The exhibition lasted for four days, but exhibitors could take their dogs home each evening on leaving one pound deposit. This was forfeited if the dog was not returned by 8.00 am the following morning. Throughout the exhibition, dogs were fed and attended to free of charge to the exhibitor.

During the 1870s the breed went from strength to strength and many fine St Bernards were produced. One of the most famous was Bayard, the property of Mr F J Smith from

Sheffield. He was a grandson of Thor on both sides of his pedigree, and won numerous championships. His great-great-grandmother was said to have been a Mastiff, and he sometimes passed Mastiff colouring to his offspring.

Unfortunately, at this point, weight and size in the breed began to take precedence over soundness and type. High prices were obtained from America for the 'giants' of the British show ring. Plinlimmon was sold for $7000 to an actor, Mr Emmett, who exhibited him in theatres. Another of the giants, Sir Bedivere, who weighed 96.2kg (212lb) and stood 85cm (33½in) at the shoulder, went to America for £1300. He finally met his match in another British export, Princess Florence, who was reported to weigh 5kg (11lb) more. Very few of the high-priced stock sent to America survived for very long, but whether this was due to the

Ch Save.

climate being too hot for them or because of their great weight is a matter for conjecture.

A Standard of Points was drawn up in 1886 by Rev Arthur Carter and Mr Frederick Gresham. It failed to halt the decline in quality that took place during the closing years of the last century. When beauty and soundness took second place to size, the breed began to lose its appeal to the public. The essential benevolent expression began to disappear, and faulty conformation, especially in the hindquarters, became common. An over-short muzzle led to breathing difficulties, but was favoured as a way of giving the impression of width and depth to the foreface.

At the turn of the century a small group of breeders rebelled against the craze for size at the expense of soundness. A Rough dog, Pouf, a small compact animal, was much used at stud, producing sounder offspring, some of whom inherited his more typical head and muzzle. The Smooth Swiss-bred bitch Belline produced Ch Guide and Ch Sans Peur, and her grandchildren included the famous Smooth dog, Ch Watch. It was on the lines from Pouf, Belline and Ch Save that future breeders based their efforts to restore quality and eminence to the breed.

A contemporary engraving of Plinlimmon shows how difficult it was to convey the St Bernard's power, compared with the photograph below.

Ch Plinlimmon.

Chapter Three

A Century of British St Bernards

1896–1939

In 1896, Dr George Inman and Mr Ben Walmsley formed a partnership and established their famous Bowden kennels, first at Barford in Somerset and finally at Bowden Priory in Cheshire. Dr Inman is said to have crossed Kenilworth, a Smooth bitch, with a brindle Mastiff, and then crossed the progeny back to his St Bernards, with successful results. The Bowden kennels soon produced a series of winners seldom beaten in the show ring, noted for correct head type and superb soundness. No unsound animals were ever exhibited or used for breeding. Their top winners included Ch Tannhauser, a Rough

Ch Judith Inman.

with 16 CCs, and Ch Viking, a Smooth with 12 CCs. Two of their bitches, the rough Ch Judith Inman and the Smooth Ch Viola, each won 14 CCs. The Bowden kennels at one time housed 12 home-bred champions. It was written of the partnership: *This firm established a race of dogs as sound as Terriers, big and massive in size, with heads the chiselling and grandeur of which even their greatest enemies were ultimately constrained to admit. With the exception of one dog, probably, there was no trace of Mastiff, or any other alien cross. Their enormously deep, square forefaces, nice stops, beautifully chiselled skulls, pellucid eyes,*

Ch Viola, born 1900.

denoting beautiful dispositions, which all the dogs possessed, were at once the admiration and marvel of the fancy.

The Bowden partnership ended with Dr Inman's death, and the Bowden stock was sold off. In one sense, the dispersal was of benefit to the breed, as it gave new heart to other exhibitors, who for many years had been overshadowed by the Bowden dominance.

One of the greatest successes of this period fell to Ch The Pride of Sussex, winner of 23 CCs, who in 1912 was Best in Show (BIS) at Crufts and Birmingham. This famous Rough dog was a son of Ch Lord Montgomery, who was by the noted Ch Tannhauser. His owner, Mr H Stockden, writing in 1913, defended the breed against accusations of deterioration: *Well, I have heard a lot about the deterioration of this breed, but, in my opinion it is in as good a way now as it has ever been since I have been exhibiting... If the breed has so deteriorated then all other breeds must be very bad indeed, and I think we can safely leave these 'croakers' to get what consolation they can out of this... At the present time the dogs exhibited are, with a few exceptions, sound, and when I started exhibiting they were just the opposite. I well remember a remark I heard made at the ringside by an onlooker that they wanted 'a wheelbarrow to bring the dogs into the ring!' This cannot be said at the present time, and is one of the reasons the breed is holding its own.*

CHAMPION.

The Pride of Sussex.

The Property of Mr. H. STOCKEN and Miss F. SAMUEL.
The best known St. Bernard of the day.

A famous rough St Bernard.

Some of the Bowden dogs found their way to the celebrated Pearl kennel of Mr and Mrs Redwood, one of the few kennels to survive World War I. This war hit the breed hard, as food was scarce, and only a nucleus of Saints remained when breeding operations recommenced. Mr and Mrs Redwood continued to breed many winners and 42 champions carried their affix. Head type did not improve during this period.

The Abbotspass Kennels (see photograph on page 34) were established in 1922 by

Ch Lord Montgomery, 1906.

Mrs K Staines at Reigate in Surrey, and her kennel buildings were claimed to be the finest in the country. Her foundation stock included Ch Bernado and Nerissa, litter-mates, bred by Mr E Chasty (Ch St Benedick Pearl ex Ch The King's Daughter). Mrs Staines was determined to get away from the Pearl strain and start a new line, and her first major success was Ch Bassanio. She imported new bloodlines from Switzerland. Her most noted winner was Ch Abbotspass Romeo, for whom she was said to have refused offers of up to £2000.

The only adult male ever to be sold by Mrs Staines was Ch Abbotspass Friar, who was acquired by Mr Horace Mellor. This dog was line-bred to Ch Sebastian Pearl, a descendant of the Bowden line. Apart from some of the noted Abbotspass dogs, the standard of the breed during the 1920s and early 1930s was generally low, and it was said that a dog at that time might be a complete cripple yet win the highest honours. Mrs Staines did not place her dogs at public stud, and so did little to improve the breed outside her own kennel. In accordance with instructions in her will, all her St Bernards were destroyed immediately after her death, so the Abbotspass blood was lost completely.

A Pearl St Bernard with owner, Mr Redwood.

On one occasion a group of contemporary breeders very much wished to use one of the Abbotspass champions. The good lady was known to have a kennelman who was somewhat overfond of his liquor, so the said breeders took the trouble to discover the whereabouts of his favourite 'local' and waylaid him there. After plying him with drink they persuaded him to agree to an illicit union, which took place next morning during a detour on his walk with the dogs. Puppies were duly born and bore such a striking resemblance to their famous sire that Mrs Staines discovered the truth and sacked the kennelman.

Ch Sabrina Pearl, 1927.

An impression of the quality of the breed at a time in the past beyond living memory can only be gained from the writings of breeders active at that time or from photographs. Bearing in mind that authors were often drawn from amongst the top exhibitors of the day, their impartiality is sometimes open to question. Photographs are unreliable evidence as well, as the impression given depends so much on the pose of the dog and the angle from which the photograph is taken, but in sufficient quantities they can show trends in the degree of conformity with essential breed points, especially where the heads are concerned. Some of the top winners of the 1920s and 1930s appear to have lacked rise and roundness of skull, definition of stop, and depth of muzzle. They also show weak pasterns and splay feet. It has been said that the Pearl dogs were usually photographed in long grass... for obvious reasons!

Future bloodlines were greatly affected by the efforts of the Misses Pratt, who established their Berndean kennels at Newton Mearns in Renfrewshire in the early 1930s. They had inherited a fortune and decided to spend it on St Bernards. They imported several Saints from Switzerland and, in 1932, mated their imported bitch, Emira Flora, to Ch Moorgate Masterpiece. This mating produced Berndean Ailsa (see page 35), an almost all-white bitch, and the rough dog, Ch The Marquis of Wetterhorn. A further mating of Ailsa, this time to Mrs Briggs' Ch Beldene Bruno, produced Ch Berndean Invader.

Of equal importance was the Pratts' importation of the

Ch Bernado, 1922. Photo: Thomas Fall.

Ch Abbotspass Friar, 1928. Photo: Thomas Fall.

Ch Abbotspass Portia – but with an untypical head.

Mrs Staines and her kennelmen with a group of Abbotspass Saints. Photo by Thomas Fall.

Berndean Prinz von Rigi, a Swiss dog imported by Miss Pratt.

Swiss dog, Berndean Prinz von Rigi. Mated to Monte Rosa, a daughter of St Silverias Pearl, he produced Jupiter of Priorsleigh, owned by Mrs N Cox of Stockport, Cheshire. A second mating of Monte Rosa, this time to The Alpine Colossus, gave rise to Fabius of Priorsleigh. The pedigrees of most of the immediate post-war St Bernards, when the great Cornagarth and Peldartor kennels dominated the breed, can be traced back to these two Priorsleigh dogs, as can be seen from the family trees in Appendix B. A high percentage

Ch Berndean Ailsa, 1935. Photo: Thomas Fall.

of Cornagarth dogs were descended in the male line from Jupiter, and the Peldartor dogs predominantly went back to Fabius.

1947–1970

Although scarcity of food during World War II meant that only a small nucleus of breeders managed to maintain their kennels, the breed was soon re-established when hostilities ceased. Among the first to come to the fore were the Boystown Saints of Mrs Graydon Bradley (see photograph on page 36), whose kennels near Dover had been destroyed by a shell during the Blitz. The Boystown dogs were noted for their magnificent heads and benign temperament, and their owner was a true Saint lover, regarded in the breed with great respect and affection. She worked closely with Scottish breeder, Miss J Fyffe.

The first post-war champion was Yew Tree St Christopher, a grandson of Jupiter of Priorsleigh on the sire's side and Ch Berndean Invader on the dam's. He was the first of 61 British champions to be made up by Mr and Mrs Gaunt, of whom almost half were home-bred.

The Gaunts of Ripley in Derbyshire (see page 38) had begun breeding St Bernards in the mid-1930s under the affix Twokays, which they later changed to Cornagarth. Their first bitch champion, bred by Mr T Lightfoot, was Cornagarth Wendy of Flossmere, a daughter of Jupiter of Priorsleigh: her dam was Prudence of Priorsleigh, by Ch Berndean Invader. Mr A K Gaunt was Secretary of the English St Bernard Club for 27 years and exerted a dominant influence on the breed during that time. Ably assisted by his wife, Kathleen, he made the Cornagarth St Bernards world-famous, although his kennel facilities were extremely limited. Cornagarth was to the immediate post-war St Bernard what Bowden, Pearl and Abbotspass had been to successive generations in the past.

The Cornagarth dogs usually had tremendous bone and good head properties. Temperament was first class, but some were not as strong in hindquarters as could have been wished. The Swiss dog, Marshall von Zwing Uri, was acquired by the Gaunts in 1952, having been brought into the country by a returning serviceman, and his name appeared in many pedigrees. During the late 1950s, the Gaunts worked in close co-operation with Mrs Gwen Slazenger, of Powerscourt in Eire. Her original affix was Thornebarton, later changed to Durrowabbey, and 11 champions carried the joint Cornagarth–Durrowabbey affix.

The other notable kennel of the early post-war years belonged to Mrs R L Walker of Thringstone in Leicestershire. Mrs Walker had owned St Bernards since the end of the last century, and began to show her dogs soon after the war ended. Her first champion was St Dominic of Brenchley, and a series of 18 others followed, almost all home-bred. With the help of her twin sons, Gilbert and Eric, she produced in her Peldartor kennels a number of tall, powerful dogs with outstanding heads and muzzles. Mrs Walker's favourites were the Smooth dog, Ch Colossus of Peldartor, and the Rough bitch, Ch Carol of Peldartor (page 38), whose son, Ch Peldartor Orrangit (page 39), was Best of Breed (BOB) at Crufts in 1956. Movement in this kennel was again something of a problem.

The Boystowns at home in 1950. Ch Glamour Girl is on the left.

Mrs Walker died in 1981 at the age of 95, both her sons having predeceased her by just a few months. Gilbert Walker had been Secretary of the United St Bernard Club for 17 years, and in this capacity did much to encourage new exhibitors. Model making and pottery were his hobbies and many examples of his work were given as souvenirs to exhibitors. The model for a number of Gilbert Walker's ceramics was Ch Peldartor Charnwood Bruno, who had been bred by the monks of the nearby Mount St Bernard Abbey, in Charnwood Forest (see photograph on page 40). This is a Cistercian community, unconnected with the Augustinian fathers at the Hospice in Switzerland. In the 1950s St Bernards were bred here and enjoyed some success in the show ring. The dogs were in the special care of the Bursar, Father Wilfred Davis, who made a special study of the breed.

Fabius of Priorsleigh and Jupiter of Priorsleigh, owned by Miss Cox.

Altrincham Show, 1937.

The noted Burtonswood kennel of Miss M Hindes came to the fore in the later 1950s. Her first champion of many was Prima Donna of Burtonswood, a daughter of Ch Peldartor Charnwood Bruno, and her many winners in the years that followed excelled in type and soundness.

An account of the Saint scene in the 1960s would not be complete without mention of the Snowranger kennels of Mrs C Bradley and Mr P Hill, who imported stock from Europe to improve their strain. From Switzerland came Ch Tello von Sauliamt, and from Holland Ch Snowranger Bas von der Vrouwenpolder. Tello was the sire of Ch Snowranger Chloris, made up in 1967.

The Bernmont kennel of the late Mrs E Muggleton and her daughter Miss P Muggleton was well-known during this period, making up several champions, among them the noted

Above: Ch Carol of Peldartor, 1952.
Top: A K Gaunt in 1947 with Ch Cornagarth Wendy of Flossmere and Ch Yew Tree St Christopher.

Ch Peldartor Orrangit, 1956.

Ch Bernmont Warlord, who won the Working Group at Bath in 1969. Miss Muggleton is the current Secretary of the English St Bernard Club.

In 1969, Mr Michael Gilbey imported into quarantine an in-whelp bitch from Germany, Gundi von Birkenkopf, who had been mated to Alex von Pava. After rearing her puppies, the bitch returned to her owners in Germany. One dog in her litter became Ch Karro von Birkenkopf, in the ownership of Mrs D Ayckbourne, who also purchased his brother, King, and one of his sisters. Mr Gaunt purchased Kuno von Birkenkopf and used him extensively at stud. He proved a much-needed outcross, bringing increased

Ch Cornagarth Marshall von Zwing Uri, 1950.

vigour, substance, height and improvement in hindquarters to the breed in this country. He sired 11 champions, all to bitches of Cornagarth or Burtonswood breeding. His influence on the breed cannot be over-estimated, and the 1970s therefore marked a new era in the development of St Bernards in this country.

Brother Alban of the Mount St Bernard Abbey, with Monberno Belle and Beldene Ajax.

1970–1979

For at least the first two years of this period, the Cornagarth and Burtonswood kennels continued to dominate the breed. In 1971, three of today's exhibitors made up their first champions: these were Michael Braysher with Burtonswood Big Time and Cornagarth Mirabelle, Maureen Gwilliam with Cornagarth Marquisite, and Bruce Everall with Ghyllendale Aristocrat. The same year saw the last Peldartor champion in Mrs Walker's Peldartor Zigismund.

The following year, our own Lindenhall High Commissioner gained his title and the first of his 15 CCs. He was the first of Kuno's offspring to be made up. His dam, Cornagarth Adelaide, had proved a very lucky purchase. My husband and I had been to look at some

Ch Cornagarth Fleur, 1972.

puppies at a house near Maidstone, and the owners offered to sell us the mother because they could not manage her. She had just been through the glass front door for the third time! She produced five champions in her litter to Kuno.

In 1972, Ken Gaunt made up the last of his 61 Cornagarth champions, the bitch Ch Cornagarth Fleur and the dog Ch Cornagarth Burtonswood Be Great. Both were offspring of Ch Cornagarth Stroller, who had been used as the model for the ceramic model of a St Bernard made by 'Beswick'. Stroller was one of

Mrs Gaunt's favourites, and she usually handled him in the ring.

In 1973 four more of Kuno's offspring gained their titles, three of them bred and owned by Miss Marjorie Hindes. One was the famous Ch Burtonswood Bossy Boots, who won BIS at Crufts the following year. He and his kennel mate, Ch Burtonswood Black Tarquin, each won 13 CCs.

Ch Lindenhall High Commissioner, 1972. Photo: Thomas Fall.

The publicity given to the success of Bossy Boots brought about a tremendous surge in the popularity of the breed. Registrations rose from 376 in 1970 to a peak of 988 in 1979. A sudden influx of this kind is bad for any breed when it stems from the desire of breeders to cash in on increased demand rather than to improve the breed. To keep pace with increased registrations, The Kennel Club boosted the numbers of CCs available to the breed. They rose from

Ch Cornagarth Burtonswood Be Great.
Photo: Diane Pearce.

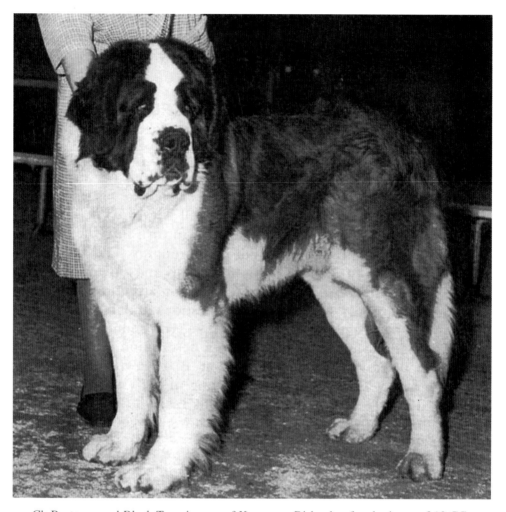

Ch Burtonswood Black Tarquin, son of Kuno von Birkenkopf and winner of 13 CCs.

14 in 1969 to a peak of 33 in 1989. This was far too many and may have contributed to a gradual deterioration in quality as there were not enough experienced judges to hand them out. Smaller entries at individual shows also resulted, reducing the level of competition. Savage and indiscriminate cuts have now been made, with six sets being axed at a stroke in 1996.

Scottish breeders enjoyed great success in the 1970s. In 1974 Mrs J McMurray won Crufts Working Group with Ch Snowranger Cascade, and the following year Mr and Mrs Whitelaw's home-bred Ch Pittforth Angus gained Best of Breed.

Four of the five champions made up in 1975 were of our Lindenhall breeding, including Mrs E Ridley's Ch Lindenhall Calamity Jane, who won 11 CCs. The other was Ch Cornagarth Cara, owned by Mrs Topping, whose Topvalley kennel enjoyed much success in the years that followed. Her Ch Topvalley Wogans Winner won a total of 19 CCs.

In November 1975, the St Bernard Club of Scotland held its first Championship Show, with Mrs Clare Bradley of Snowranger fame awarding BIS to our Smooth, Ch Lindenhall Capability Brown. Mrs McMurray was then Secretary to the Scottish Club, and what a success she made of it!

The year 1976 saw the first of the home-bred Whaplode dogs achieve success. Mr and Mrs John Harpham's Ch Whaplode Desdemona gained her title, as did Mrs and Miss Muggleton's Ch Whaplode Eros of Bernmont. The Whaplode kennel has produced a series of noted winners, including the breed's bitch record holder, Ch Lucky Charm of Whaplode, who won 24 CCs during her show career. Whaplode dogs are still prominent in the ring, now ably handled by Mrs Mary Pearl, daughter to Mr and Mrs Harpham. Their Ch Whaplode Be Our William currently holds 40 CCs. The Harphams are the only present-day breeders who have produced the correct St Bernard head type consistently, together with size and substance. They have done this cleverly, without recourse to continental outcrosses which, although they may have improved hindquarters marginally, have in some cases done little for type and temperament.

In 1977 Mr and Mrs Wensley made up their first champion, the bitch Benem Lady Guinevere, who came from a good litter by Lucky Strike of Cornagarth, out of a Kuno bitch. They have produced a series of fine-headed dogs in their Swindridge kennels, including several impressive Smooths. Another top winner from the Lucky Strike litter was Ch Benem Sir Galahad, owned by Mrs Joy Evans of the Hartleapwell St Bernards. In the 1980s she bred four champions in a litter (Ch Whaplode My Lord ex Ch Hartleapwell Magic Moments). Mrs Evans' dogs were always immaculately presented and expertly handled.

Three early Whaplode champions: Desdemona (1976), Ivanhoe (1978) and Unique (1980).

Ch Hartleapwell Midnite Magic, at home with Jody.

Towards the end of the 1970s, Bossy Boots' offspring began to make their mark in the ring. He sired 15 champions, 12 of them male, and is behind the pedigrees of many of today's top winners.

1980–1997

A notable winner at the beginning of the 1980s was Mrs Sue Roberts' bitch Ch Roddinghead Agent Kris of Knockespoch who won 10 CCs and BOB at Crufts. She passed her lovely type on to two of her daughters, Ch Lucky Charm of Whaplode and Ch Knockespoch Berenice, both by Ch Whaplode Unique. In 1981, Mr and Mrs Boulden made Burtonswood Black Duke up to champion, and various others have followed, including Lady Prudence of Middlepark, a daughter of Ch Benem Sir Galahad in 1983. This kennel has recently produced some excellent smooths, among them litter brother and sister Ch Middlepark Meridian and Ch Middlepark Lettice. Their latest Rough champion, Middlepark Araminter, won two CCs while still a puppy.

The Ravensbank kennel of Mrs P Stammers made up Ravensbank Hard Time in 1982. Her kennel mate, Ravensbank Simply Solomen at Sileeda, was sold to the late Mrs Rosemary Hoyle, who won two CCs with him. When she disbanded her kennels, 'Solly' returned to his breeder and had a successful stud career, as today's pedigrees show.

In 1984, Mr and Mrs P Girling bred Ch Schnozzer Huggy Bear and Mr and Mrs H W Lux made up Ch Bernadino Maxi, the first of three title holders from a litter by Ch Topvalley Wogan's Winner.

In the following year, three more kennels achieved top honours. Mr and Miss E Cooper made up Ch Merridale Bouncer and won the Working Group at Bath with him. When Mrs Sue Roberts disbanded her kennels, the Coopers took over stock from the good Knockespoch bitch line, so it was not completely lost. That same year, John, May and Helen Bateman scored with Ch Knockespoch Highline and Miss Thomas and Mr Churchill made up Finetime Sardonyx, the first of a number of Finetime champions.

Miss P Muggleton's German import Pankraz von den Drei Helman of Bernmont gained his title in 1986, as did Mrs L Martin's Marlender Moonraker and, from Scotland, Mr and Mrs R Gardner's Treeburn Challenger.

In 1988 Mr John Taylor won top honours with the litter brother and sister Earl of Alvaston and My Lucky Lady. They were the first champion offspring from Ch Finetime the Great Bear.

The following year Mr and Mrs Bateman won with their Swedish import Ch Bernegardens JR of Fastacre. Other imports from the Bernegardens kennel of Brit Halvorsen have followed, and their long-term influence on the breed has still to be shown.

Mrs Deuchar Fawcett's bitch, Saranbeck Sweep, became a champion in 1989, and she recently had the honour of breeding the only St Bernard to win BOB at Crufts twice, namely Mrs L Martin's Ch Saranbeck Sayra at Marlender. One of Mrs Fawcett's latest champions, Saranbeck Smugglers Gold, is granddaughter to an imported Dutch bitch, Esther v Irsteanjo Hof, brought into this country by Mrs Fawcett in 1988.

Also in 1989 Mr and Mrs Byles' Ch Lynbern Dennis the Menace of Meadowmead burst upon the show scene and, during a brilliant career, amassed a total of 39 CCs, making him the present breed record holder. He was a grandson of Ch Topvalley Karl, bred by Mrs Winn (Ravensbank Simply Solomen at Sileeda ex Finetime Solar System).

The first half of the 1990s was notable for successes by bitches from the excellent Mountside line. Coatham Britania (Ch Schnozzer Huggy Bear ex Ch Coatham Hermes) was bred by Mrs Gwilliam and owned by Mr and Mrs Stokell of Mountside kennels, Hexham. She was mated twice to Ch Finetime the Great Bear, one litter producing the bitch Mountside Moonshine, who was the dam of Mrs MacLaughlan's Ch Mountside Serenade at Culrain. From the second litter came Ch Mountside Movie Star (who had two champion daughters by Finetime Brother Gabriel), Mr and Mrs Simpson's Ch Mountside Secret of Campsie, and Mrs McMurray's Ch Mountside Starlight at Alpentire. Britania's litter to Ravensbank Simply Solomen at Sileeda gave rise to Mr and Mrs Byles' Ch Mountside Mauritania of

Ch Middlepark Araminter, owned by Mrs Boulden. Photo: Carol Ann Johnson.

Ch Middlepark Meridian
(Ch Timeside Mr Sloba-Doba ex
Middlepark Gabriella).

Meadowmead and to another bitch, Mountside Melody. Melody was mated to Ch Dragonville Lord Snooty at Coatham and gave birth to Mr and Mrs Davis' Ch Mountside Solitaire, who was the dam of their Ch Timeside Mr Sloba-Doba, top winning Saint in 1995. Sloba-Doba has already sired two champions in one litter by Middlepark Gabriella. A good example of line breeding and quite a record! When the Mountside kennel was disbanded, Ch Movie Star went to Mrs Gwilliam's Coatham kennel. She had no more puppies, but won a total of 22 CCs and was BOB at Crufts in 1994.

During the 1990s there have been further infusions of continental blood, notably from the Swedish kennel of Brit Halvorsen. Mr and Mrs Goodwin imported Norwegian Ch Bernegardens Buckpasser in 1990 and he gained his title in this country the following year. Several other importations from the same kennel have taken place. One of Buckpasser's sons, Ch Abbotsbury

Impression, was made up in 1994, and his grandson, Ch Abbotsbury Ailanthus, was top winner at Crufts in 1996.

Another top winner of the 1990s was Jill and Werner Lux's Smooth, Ch Winterburg's Boy, who won 17 CCs including Crufts in 1990. Miss Barbara Swaine-Williams' Ch Coatham Good News for Wyandra, bred by Maureen and George Gwilliam, had a successful show career, going BIS at two breed club events, the Eastern in 1992 and the United in 1994. As I have already said, Ch Whaplode

Ch Bernadino Maxi (1984). Owned and bred by Jill and Werner Lux. Photo: Martin Leigh.

Ch Mountside Movie Star, winning BOB at Crufts 1994.

Be Our William, owned and bred jointly by John and Mary Harpham and Mrs Mary Pearl, currently has 40 CCs. Both he and Ch Coatham Good News for Wyandra are sons of Mr and Mrs Girling's Ch Schnozzer Latest Edition.

It seems at the time of writing that the type of the breed in this country is moving away from what used to be the accepted interpretation of the standard. In some show classes it is difficult to find two Saints of similar head type. Short broad muzzles are the exception, skulls are becoming too narrow, and eyes get lighter all the time. The loose skin on the forehead which, when too profuse, hung over the eyes and led to entropion (see chapter 13), has decreased in many specimens, but now we have plain heads with little suggestion of the 'wrinkle'

which gave the dog expression when alert. There may be less entropion now but clean eyes are a rarity.

The correct ear set, with well-developed burr, has all but disappeared, giving the impression of narrow skulls. Height and bone are wanting in some specimens, and movement is still faulty in too many exhibits. Most serious of all is the loss in some cases of the lovely gentle temperament for which our breed in this country was once noted.

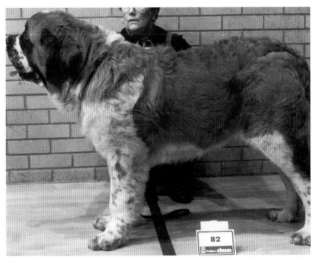

Ravensbank Simply Solomen at Sileeda
at seven months. Photo: Tony Reed.

Chapter Four

St Bernards Worldwide

Although this is primarily a book about British St Bernards, it would not be complete without a brief summary of the Saint scene elsewhere in the world. For obvious reasons, the St Bernard is universally popular, and it would be impossible to describe in detail the developments of the breed overseas and the various types currently favoured elsewhere in the world. In any case, lists of breeders and the names of their dogs are of little significance unless supported by photographs of the animals mentioned. Overseas breeders and clubs have been most helpful in supplying photographic records for this chapter, and their help has been greatly appreciated, even though lack of space has meant that it has not always been possible to include all the material received.

The World Union of St Bernard Clubs

A union of St Bernard Clubs worldwide was the dream of the late Albert de la Rie. In 1967 he organised a St Bernard gathering in Switzerland, with an attendance of 200 enthusiasts from 10 different countries. Over 100 St Bernards took part in the show.

The World Union of St Bernard Clubs (WUSB) was established, and every year a WUSB Show is held in a different member country. Delegates meet annually to determine show venues and other matters concerning the breed. Members of the Union must endorse the Fédération Cynologique Internationale (FCI) standard for the breed, by which Saints are judged in Switzerland and at all WUSB shows. America seems to be an exception to this rule: the United States last hosted the WUSB show in 1993, with eight judges, including six from Europe.

In 1994 the WUSB had 12 members: Germany, Netherlands, America, Belgium, Switzerland, Finland, Norway, Denmark, Italy, France, Austria and Luxembourg. Australia has now adopted the FCI standard (in preference to the English) and has therefore been admitted to membership. It is now possible for countries which do not follow the FCI standard to become associate members of the Union and attend meetings, but without voting rights.

The current President of the WUSB is Wolfgang Ketzler, a leading German breeder and one-time Secretary of the German Club.

Australasia

St Bernards have been known in Australia since the 1880s, most early imports coming from England. In his book *The Dog in Australia* Walter Beilby reported that the first to introduce the breed was a Mr E F Stephen of Sydney, owner of Monarque III and Minerva, who won many prizes for a Mr Anderson of Kew, Victoria. Both were failures as breeding stock, and very little progress was made until other imports arrived in 1887. Many did not survive the long sea passage, or died in quarantine shortly after arrival. In 1888, 19 Saints were exhibited at Melbourne Show, and the breed gained in popularity until the end of the century, after which its numbers declined steadily.

A revival of interest began during the 1960s and numerous imports of varied quality were again sent out from Great Britain. An American bitch went to New South Wales in 1968 and her offspring to a British dog did well in the show ring. Imports from the United States followed, and frozen semen from American dogs was used by breeders to improve Australian blood lines. During the 1980s German blood was introduced.

There has been frequent interchange of stock with New Zealand and, in 1991, semen from a Swedish import to that country was utilised. Following the current emphasis on German, American and Scandinavian stock, Australia has now abandoned the use of The Kennel Club Breed Standard, opting for the more comprehensive FCI guidelines.

Western Australia

There was little show activity during the 1970s, but from 1974 to 1984 several Burtonswood Saints were imported. The 1980s saw an increase in show support, the top winner being Aust Ch D'Mowbray Star Royal, who was bred from Ch Freesea Fritz and NZ Ch Sedna I'm Sigrid. Star Royal was bought by the Sylvenus Kennels of Joan Jensen and her husband, in whose ownership he had numerous wins. Aust Ch Chrystlepark Trans Am, a grandson of Star Royal, has won BOB at Perth Royal Show for three consecutive years.

In the mid 1980s more

Aust Ch Chrystalpark Brook and Aust Ch Chrystalpark Trans Am.

German lines were introduced from Aramis v d Kurstadt, a forefather of Ch Southside Sir Konrad, who sired the top winner Ch Raaleppo Torn Amber, owned by Anne Oppelaar, and Ch Sylvenus Lylla, the property of Mr and Mrs Jensen.

The late 1980s and early 1990s saw the introduction of new bloodlines from the

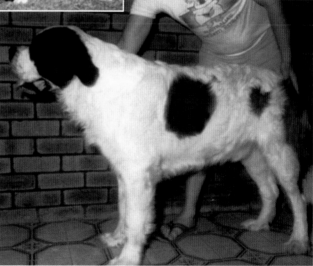

Aust Ch Southside Sir Konrad.

Aust Ch Raaleppo Torn Amber.

United States and Sweden, the American import Ch Stiniyasu Kick Boxer being the only Smooth Saint to date to be a multi Best in Group winner.

The Western Australia show ring is currently dominated by three winning bitches from the same litter by Aust Ch Raaleppo Torn Amber, out of the New Zealand-bred bitch Bernedale Lady Titene, a daughter of

Aust Ch Sylvenus Lylla.

Bernegardens Joker Adamson. Another import from New Zealand is Aust Ch Bernedale Just Conway, who has produced some outstanding Smooths and is starting to dominate the show scene. Both are owned by Anne Oppelaar of Raaleppo kennels.

The two breed clubs are the Western Australian Social Club and Welfare Association, and the St Bernard Breed Club of Western Australia. Both cater for show and

Three top winning champion bitches by Ch Raaleppo Torn Amber.
From left to right: Good Luck Charm, Flaming Star and Raised on Rock.

pet owners alike, running educational functions and well-respected Rescue Services. Breeders and exhibitors strive to produce quality St Bernards and encourage owners to X-ray hips and elbows and guarantee their puppies.

Tasmania

There has been documented evidence of the presence of St Bernards in this island state of Australia since the 1890s. At a show in 1894 organised by the Tasmanian Poultry and Dog Society, 11 of those shown gained places. The best Saint was Mr J Sykes' Jumbo XI, bred in Adelaide.

Aust Ch Tremel Distant Saint, owned by John, Judy and Susan Teniswood of Tasmania.

By 1907, show entries had started to dwindle, and a local newspaper lamented, *A show without these magnificent specimens to top it up is very vacant!*

During the late 1930s there was a slight revival, with a Mr Raymond Scott exhibiting. In 1955 he imported two Cornagarth dogs from Great Britain. The breed in Tasmania became more popular during the 1970s, with imports arriving from mainland Australia, New Zealand and Great Britain. The St Bernard Social Club of Tasmania was formed in 1981 to promote and assist the breed. As it is not fully affiliated to the ANKC it is unable to hold Championship Shows, but many other events are organised.

Mr and Mrs Johnson of Lympne Kennels imported two Whaplode dogs in the early

1980s, and another was brought in by Mr Sayer of Mymaggie Kennels. Two Maurbry Saints, bred by Mrs Chapman, came to the Averyhill Kennels of Mr and Mrs Flockart.

In 1983, Mr and Mrs J Teniswood purchased Aust Ch Tremel Distant Saint (photograph page 51) from Cornish breeders Mr and Mrs S Haywood, and Mr and Mrs Burn of Actongold Kennels brought in his litter sister, Aust Ch Tremel Faraway Lady.

Three bitches from New Zealand's Bernedale Kennels were imported in 1995, all were from different litters by the Swedish-bred NZ Ch Bernegardens Khedive. Much Scandinavian stock has recently reached New Zealand. Two

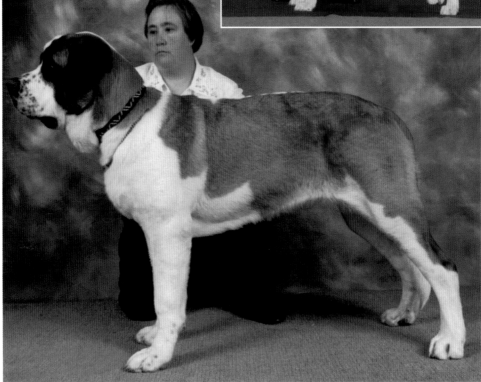

Above: Aust Ch Boroniahil Monza. Photo: Robin Twigg.
Top: Aust/NZ Ch Chenalette Golden Rule. Photo: Steve Mathie.

other imports from New Zealand to reach the Teniswood's Boroniahil Kennels have been Aust/NZ Ch Chenalette Golden Rule and Chenalette High Stepper.

Aust Ch Tremel Distant Saint had a brilliant show career in Australia, going BIS in 1985 at The Royal Hobart Show. Golden Rule already has a BIS award in Tasmania and is currently being campaigned by his breeders in New Zealand, where he has won another two All Breeds BIS awards. Both dogs have produced many champions, and feature in the pedigrees of winning St Bernards in a number of Australian states.

The St Bernards of Mr and Mrs W Bald have had great success in the ring. Their Aust Ch Lapusca Kossie Osco and Aust Ch Lapusca Big Time (both bred by Mrs E Burke) won many All Breeds BIS Awards. Aust Ch Southerton Katarina, a daughter of Kossie Osca bred by the Balds, won BIS at the Royal Launceston Show in 1993. These three Saints won BOB at the Royal Melbourne Show (Australia's largest) for a number of years. In 1996, Aust Ch Lapusca Big Time went BIS at the St Bernard Club of Victoria Championship Show.

New South Wales and Victoria
The St Bernard Club of NSW was formed in 1976 and held its first Championship Show in 1978. Best in Show was Aust Ch Freesea Claudius, bred in Australia from Buta St Jeremy and Lindenhall the Joker. Best bitch went to an English import, My Lady Emma, a daughter of Kuno von Birkenkopf and dam of Mr and Mrs R Miller's Benem litter in Great Britain.

The Portway Saints are owned by Phillipa and Ian Clark, who have been active in the breed for 25 years, and published the comprehensive *St Bernard Annual* during the early 1990s.

Ian Clark with Aust Ch Portway Man of Colours.

Their current top winner is Aust Ch Portway Man of Colours, who has won 75 CCs during his outstanding show career. He was named Number One Saint Australasia in 1995 by OZDOG newspaper. Man of Colours has a hip score of 10 (6:4) and chilled semen from him has been used in several other Australian states. His first progeny are already making their mark in the ring. His two sisters are also champions, the litter being line-bred to the German import Aramis von der Kursdadt, who had such a marked influence on the breed throughout Australia. Also notable have been the progeny of Aust Ch Leighpark Gentle John, bred in Victoria and owned by Bob and Di Holdsworth of Hollylodge Kennels.

Modern foundations of the breed were laid by the Misses Chisman, who imported several British Saints bred in the Dale End kennels during the 1960s. In 1975 they brought out Cornagarth Chiquita in whelp to Ch Burtonswood Bossy Boots.

Mr and Mrs Ormsby owned the Paxis kennels of New South Wales. Their top winner was Aust Ch Daneeal Targus, the offspring of an American bitch and Ch Karl of Cornagarth, who had been bred in Great Britain by Michael Braysher from Kuno von Birkenkopf and Ch Burtonswood Big Time. Karl was imported by Mrs Briggs of the Snowsaint Kennels in Victoria.

Above: Aust Ch Hollylodge Rockford.   Top: Aust Ch Corocholi Gem Jacinta.

NZ Grand Ch and Aust Ch Hollylodge Tiny Tot, record winner of over 150 CCs.

The Merribuff Saints of Mrs Bridges and Mrs Dowsey have had much success in Victoria. They imported Ch Whaplode Great Expectations from Mr and Mrs Harpham. In 1977 Alpentire Klara Bow went from Mrs J McMurray's kennels in whelp to our Ch Lindenhall Capability Brown and produced top winners at Melbourne and Sydney in 1978. Klara Bow's later mating to the American import Big Ben Schwarzwald Hofiv produced the top-winning bitch Aust Ch Merribuff Inga von Banz. The Merribuff kennels have continued their winning ways to this day, with Aust Ch Merribuff Liberty's Vicar winning Best in Group and Reserve BIS at Adelaide Royal Show in 1994.

New Zealand
New Zealand has two St Bernard Clubs, both formed in 1979, and now each holding two

Aust Ch Merribuff Liberty's Vicar, top winner, 1995. Photo: C8 Photography.

NZ Ch Tai Yuan True to Form.

annual shows. First President of The St Bernard Club Inc was the late R F Spellerberg of Christchurch, whose daughter Karen published the quarterly magazine *St Bernards in Australasia* during the 1980s. The North Island St Bernard Association Inc now has a very large membership under Secretary Charmaine Kendrick of Le Baricant kennel. The magazine *Saint Scene* is published bi-monthly. The Association's first open show was held in 1984, with Aust Ch D'Mowbray Star Courage taking the top award. A recent championship event drew an entry of 70 Saints. Smooths have increased in popularity recently, but at present there are no separate classes for them.

New Zealand at present judges its Saints by the old British standard (not according to The Kennel Club's 1986 truncated version) but moves are afoot to adopt the 1961 FCI standard, like Australia.

Currently the Tai Yuan St Bernards

Three Grand Champions from the Tai Yuan Kennels. From left to right:
Tai Yuan Taste of Heaven, Tai Yuan Forever Amber and Tai Yuan Slice of Heaven.

NZ Ch Tai Yuan Iceberg, the first Saint bred in New Zealand from frozen semen.

belonging to Clyde Rogers and Cath Tippett is the most successful kennel in Australasia. They have bred more than 40 champions, with three gaining Grand Champion status. To win this title a dog must be awarded at least 50 CCs and be BIS at an All Breeds Championship Show on at least three occasions.

In 1979 Tai Yuan purchased the bitch NZ Ch Freesea Lorelei, who had been bred in Australia from Lindenhall bloodlines. She was mated to the British import NZ Ch Burtonswood Famous Boots, and a bitch from this mating, NZ Ch Tai Yuan Claudia, did well in the show ring. She gave birth to two dog puppies produced by artificial insemination from Ch Whaplode My Lord in 1984. One puppy became NZ Ch Tai Yuan Iceberg and had a major influence on the breed in New Zealand, still winning well as an eight-year-old veteran. The Tai Yuan kennel has used frozen semen successfully on two subsequent occasions, from Int Ch Bernegardens JR in 1991 and from Aust Ch Southside Little Big Man in 1995, producing quality puppies in each litter.

The Tai Yuan kennel has an excellent record at North Island Breed Club, winning BIS at the first championship event in 1986, and again in 1989, with Ch Tai Yuan Iceberg. In 1988 the honour went to their Grand Champion Hollylodge Tiny Tot, owned

NZ Ch Bernabby Man with a Plan.

Miss Robin E Reid's Can Ch Mont Blanc's Big Woofer, Canada's top dog, 1976.

in partnership with Phillip Potter and Alan Laird of the Bernabby Kennel, who repeated the win in 1990 and 1991. Bred in Victoria by Bob Holdsworth, this dog won more than 150 CCs and headed the Pal Supreme Dog Contest in 1991. The Tai Yuan Kennel won BIS at the North Island Championship Show again in 1992 with Gr Ch Tai Yuan Forever Amber.

In 1993 the Tai Yuan kennel imported NZ/Aust Ch Fastacre Cotton Duke (Int Ch Bernegardens JR of Fastacre ex Fastacre High Society) from John and May Bateman. He proved his worth as a sire before his premature death in June 1996. His progeny include NZ Ch Tai Yuan Tasman Pride and also NZ Ch Tai Yuan True to Form, winner of BIS at the North Island Championship Show in 1995, and his kennel mate, the bitch NZ Ch Tai Yuan On The Town, who took the same award in 1996 under Danish judge Carl Otto Mastrup.

Tim and Joy Harvey started to breed St Bernards under the affix Bernedale seven years ago. They have imported a number of Saints from Sweden's Bernegardens kennel, including NZ Champions Bernegardens Lachesis, Bernegardens Khedive and Bernegardens Joker Adamson, the latter in conjunction with Judith O'Leary.

Malcolm and Ann Simmons of the Chenalette kennel have also imported from Sweden.

They are currently campaigning a home-bred son of Gr Ch Hollylodge Tiny Tot, Aust/NZ Ch Chenalette Golden Rule, owned by the Teniswoods of Tasmania.

The Sanctum Grove kennel of Tony and Vickie Hill and the Neuchalet of Karen Fuller have also had good results from the use of frozen semen from the United States of America.

Charmaine Kendrick's Le Baricant kennel has bred 11 New Zealand champions and is currently campaigning a daughter of NZ Ch Fastacre Cotton Duke out of their home-bred champion Le Baricant Emerald Isle.

The Snowpeak kennel of Alan and Sue Stretton won well at the Pal National Dog Show in September 1996 with their litter brother and sister NZ Ch Snowpeak Alpine Lad and NZ Ch Snowpeak Alpine Lass. The dog went BOB and finally was judged BIS. His sister won well in Obedience and was Best Saint Bitch.

North America

The United States of America

St Bernards are amongst the 10 most popular breeds in the United States with registrations exceeding 35,000 annually. There are at least 30 regional St Bernard Clubs, and show classes attract large entries. The presentation is an object lesson, with many dogs being professionally handled. American Saints tend to be smaller and lighter in bone than those in Great Britain, and many are smooth-haired. The American Kennel Club St Bernard standard is based on the FCI standard, and has been adopted by the St Bernard Club of America.

Mr and Mrs John Gauthier's Can Ch Arlberg's Grand Taurus, 1977.

The first American Saints were those exported from Great Britain in the 1880s to the actor J K Emmett, who exhibited them on stage and at fairs. Early breeders concentrated on size rather than type, and so many unsound dogs were produced that interest waned.

The breed again became popular in the 1920s, due largely to the efforts of Joseph Fleischli, of the Edelweiss Kennel in Springfield, Illinois. He imported stock from Germany and Switzerland and revived the Breed Club, founded in 1880, which had become defunct due to lack of interest. Other well-known early breeders were Mr and Mrs Hayes, who imported from Switzerland to build up their Alpine Plateau strain.

Many of the pre-war imports were Roughs but, after hostilities ceased, the importance of the Smooth cross in breeding programmes became apparent, and many Smooths were brought in from Europe.

The show system in America differs greatly from that in this country. There are General (All Breed) Shows and Specialty Shows, which are confined to one breed. The St Bernard Club of America holds an annual National Specialty Show and most of the numerous regional St Bernard Clubs hold their own Specialty Shows. Specialty Shows run by different breed clubs are sometimes held at the same venue on consecutive days, an arrangement which suits the professionals who handle the dogs.

Mr and Mrs D Patterson's Am/Can Ch St Marco's Royal Frost, 1988.

Mr and Mrs Jim Wright's Am/Can Ch Swissview Simon Says, 1994.

At all shows there are five regular breed classes, divided by sex. They are Puppy, Novice, Bred by Exhibitor, American Bred, and Open. It is compulsory for winners of these regular classes to compete in what are known as The Winners Classes, one for each sex. Championship points are awarded for Best Winners Dog and Best Winners Bitch, in accordance with a scale laid down by the American Kennel Club, which is based on the number of entries and the number of dogs competing. Points never exceed 5 at any one show, and 15 must be won at shows under three different judges to make a dog a champion. An added complication is that a 3–5 Point win is classed as a Major, and two Majors under two different judges are needed for Champion status. Dogs that have already gained their titles may not compete in Winners Classes, but may challenge for BOB. This must make it easier for dogs to gain their titles than in Great Britain, where it is possible for an outstanding dog to go on winning CCs after gaining its title, so excluding its rivals.

With such a complex organisation and so many breed clubs, it is impossible to give details of more than a very few top kennels. One such is the Sanctuary Woods Kennel of Mrs Beatrice Knight of Oregon. Mrs Knight started her kennels in 1948 and has dedicated her life to her Saints and the improvement of the breed.

Laurence Powell's St Bernards are behind some of America's top show dogs today. He started his Powell kennel at the beginning of the 1940s, based on Alpine Plateau stock, and bred numerous top winners. His first great dog was Am Ch King Laddie Rasko Whitebread, who was BOB at Westminster Championship Show in 1946 and was named Dog of the Year for all breeds. Mr Powell was a skilled handler and always campaigned his own dogs in the ring. He and his contemporary, Herman Peabody of the Brownhelm Saints, were much in demand as judges of the breed, as is Donna Buxton of the Twin Oaks Kennels, who works her dogs in Obedience.

Another very famous kennel was that of Lillian and William Buell of the Subira St Bernards. Their bitch, Ch Nelda of Birchwood, bred 22 champions including the famous Am Ch Subira's Casper the Viking, who won a total of 127 BOBs, which is believed to be a record for any Saint.

Marlene and Douglas Anderson of Pennsylvania started their Beau Cheval Kennels in 1961 and have made up over 50 champions.

The top kennel of the 1990s is Glenn Radcliff's and Richard Steinberger's Opdyke St Bernards. These breeders are currently carrying all before them in the show ring. Their Am Ch Opdyke's Stetson was BOB at the National Specialty Show in 1994. At the same show, Caravan's Ellicott of Opdyke won Winners Dog and Opdyke's Eden took Winners Bitch and Best of Winners. Am Ch Osage's Amanda of Twin Oaks, part owned by Donna Buxton, was Best Opposite Sex. All these dogs were rough-coated. Two Opdyke St Bernards have recently been imported into Great Britain and their offspring have yet to make their presence felt in the ring.

In 1996, the St Bernard Club of America National Specialty Show, held at Frederick, Maryland, drew an entry of 198 Saints. Since the show was held in the eastern part of the USA, many dogs from the West Coast were unable to attend. Best of Breed was five-year-old dog Am Ch Lynch Creeks Executive, owned by Clyde and Cathy Dunphy and bred by Candy Blancher in Washington. Best Opposite Sex was 18-month-old Am Ch Cache Retreat Academy, bred and owned by Ivan Palmblad.

Canada

The first St Bernards to reach Canada came almost entirely from Great Britain and the United States of America. Interest was strong at the time of the First World War, when the bitch Lady Carlisle, a granddaughter of Ch Democrat of Dufferyn, was sent to Manitoba from Great Britain. In the following year she was followed by Lady Wolfram, who was sent to Montreal and whose great-grandparents included British champions Tannhauser, Viola and Florentius.

In 1922 Mr and Mrs Redwood exported Sir James Pearl and Sir William Pearl to Mrs Mountain in Ontario. Further exports from Great Britain during the 1920–1930s included two daughters of Ch Berndean Invader, sent to Ontario by Mr W Barton and Mrs Cox. In 1957, A K Gaunt sent Cornagarth Mount Rosa, daughter of Ch Cornagarth Culzean Nero, to Ontario.

Many of today's Canadian St Bernards trace their origins to stock from America, behind these being imports to the States from leading continental breeders. Dual Canadian and American champions are fairly common, as there are no quarantine barriers between the two countries. Every year, the top Canadian Saint is calculated for *Dogs in Canada*, the official publication of the Canadian Kennel Club. Dogs earn one point for every dog they defeat during the year. The record is currently held by Can Ch Ambassadeur, who scored an amazing 11,361 points in 1973. He was also top dog in the Working Group.

Am/Can Ch Bernduff's Peekaboo Atlas Two, BIS at Canada's largest outdoor show.

Mrs Joyce Reid of Ontario has kindly supplied me with photographs of some of the winners of the Top Dog Award from 1976 to the present day.

In 1976 the winner was Can Ch Mont Blanc's Big Woofer (page 58), campaigned by Mrs Reid's daughter, Robin. The pedigree of his American sire included several well-known Swiss bloodlines. 'Oscar' lived as a much-loved companion to the grand old age of 12½.

The title in 1977 went to Can Ch Arlberg's Grand Taurus (page 59), bred and owned by Mr and Mrs John Gauthier of Quebec.

Top dog in 1978 was David and Toni Patterson's Canadian-bred Can Ch Jelloo's Lucifer's Lightening, with 3383 points.

Am/Can Ch Arlberg's Kondor won the coveted title five years running from 1980 to 1984 for Mr and Mrs John Gauthier. His pedigree was mainly Canadian, although his paternal great grand dam was one of Dr Morsiani's exports, Stella del Soccorso, a daughter of the famous Italian Ch Alma del Soccorso.

From 1985–87 the title went to Am/Can Ch Swissview's Charlemore, owned by Mr and Mrs Wright of Ontario. He was mainly Canadian bred, although his sire was a dual American and Canadian champion and his grandsire was the famous Can Ch Ambassadeur. The Wrights won again in 1994 with their Am/Can Ch Swissview Simon Says (page 61).

In 1988 the title again went to Mr and Mrs Patterson with their home-bred Can Ch St Marco's Royal Frost (page 60).

known Swiss Ch Castor von Leberberg, a noted stud dog, and his litter brother, Cargo von Leberberg, grandsire to Cornagarth Kuno von Birkenkopf, who had such an influence on the breed in this country. Sire to Castor and Cargo was another significant Swiss stud dog, Seiger Tyrus von Haniathaus, so Switzerland and Germany must share the credit for Kuno's successful effect on the breed in the Great Britain.

Germany

Early pioneers of the St Bernard in Germany imported stock from Great Britain and Switzerland to lay the foundations of the breed in their own country. The most famous was

Courage, a top winner in 1878 and 1882.

Dr Caster, of Winkle Rheingau, who also bred Great Danes. He was instrumental in setting up the German St Bernard Club in 1891; it originally had 60 members, many from Bavaria, and was based in Munich. Caster's kennel was not large, and he imported British dogs in preference to Swiss, as he believed that the British breeders, having paid high prices for their stock, had acquired the very best. In Caster's day, most of the German dogs were Roughs, and were known as Alpenhunde.

Prince Albrecht of Solms had one of the largest early kennels on the continent. From Great Britain he imported the Smooth dog, Courage, said to be a great show specimen but disappointing at stud. He was greyish-white with yellow patches and, although said to stand 90cm (35.5in) at shoulder, he weighed only 63.6kg (140lb), so must have been somewhat lightly built.

Thirty-six St Bernards were entered at the Hanover

German Smooth male 1995. Photo: M E Collis.

All-breed Show in 1882, but only six were considered pure-bred. The English judge placed some of the cross-breds among the winners, upsetting the German breeders. Cadwallader, an English import, was BOB, while Gessler, owned by the Prince of Solms, was placed second.

During the years following the Hanover show, St Bernards became increasingly popular in Germany, and many new breeders became involved. Indiscriminate crossing is said to have led to some fall in quality. The Altona kennel founded by Ludwig Kaston in 1897 was one of the most notable and helped the breed to survive World War I. Max Nather took over the direction of the German St Bernard Club in 1903 and was responsible for its Stud Book and publications until 1938. Many good dogs were bred in the Grossglockner Kennels of Hans Glockner, who ran the Club from 1938 to 1950, maintaining interest in the breed against great odds

Bitch and puppy, 1989. A postcard issued by the German St Bernard Club.

during World War II. Another great German breeder, Alois Schmid, learned a great deal from Glockner. His Bismarckturm St Bernards were well-known during the 1930s. His motto, *A good breeder lives for his dogs, not on them*, could be much more widely followed.

Champion German Rough male 1995.
Photo: M E Collis.

German 'Bundessieger' Int Ch Sando von Geutenreuth, 1994.

The Nazis tried to interfere with the breeding of St Bernards, as they wished the German Shepherd to be regarded as Germany's national dog. The SS printed articles criticising the eyes and shape of the St Bernard head as indicating viciousness, and the Nazis forbade the awarding of the titles Club Champion and International Champion. However, at the beginning of the war, they were only too ready to train St Bernards as rescue dogs for use in Alpine conditions.

The war and its aftermath inevitably harmed the breed greatly and, at a time when money was almost useless, St Bernards were even bartered to buy food. Like the nation itself, the breed in Germany has made a remarkable recovery, and German kennels now house some of the best dogs in Europe. With Teutonic thoroughness, the German Club places careful restrictions on the activities of its members, and these help to prevent poor breeding practices. Each dog and bitch must have a breeding licence from the club, which means that when it is at least 20 months old it must be examined by a St Bernard judge, who can certify that it complies with the standard. It must also be X-rayed for hip dysplasia (HD), the degrees of which vary from 0-4, with only 0-3 qualifying for a licence.

A bitch may be mated every nine months but, if more than six puppies are reared, the permitted mating intervals become longer. Each kennel and litter is visited by club officials, who tattoo a number into each puppy's left ear. The Club issues the pedigree, which states name, ear number, description of colour and coat, three generations of breeding and the breeder's name. Offences against these rules are punished by fines and prolongation of mating intervals. The German Breed Club is currently one of the strongest and most active in Europe, having over 1000 members.

Famous among recent winners in Germany is the Smooth Saint Int Ch Sando von Geutenreuth, who was BOB at the FCI World Show at Dortmund in 1991 and at the FCI Europe Show in 1992. He also won the German St Bernard Club Show and the World Union event. Sando is owned by Werner and Edith Moser, and was bred by Reinhold Welsch in 1989.

Ireland

The St Bernard Club of Ireland was founded in 1972. Its current Chairman is Austin Long-Doyle of the Longsdyle St Bernard kennel. Irish dogs have competed successfully in Great Britain, there being no quarantine restrictions between Eire and the United Kingdom. Likewise, several top winners in this country have qualified as champions in Ireland, so becoming entitled to add the prestigious words International Champion (Int Ch) before their names.

Dog shows in Northern Ireland are held under the control of The Kennel Club, but Eire comes under the jurisdiction of The Irish Kennel Club and has a different system of awarding championship points. To gain its title a dog must win a total of 40 championship points,

Ir Ch Meadowmead Cassandra, Annual Champion 1993 and 1995. Photo: Long-Doyle.

The Tralee Championship Show 1995.

Champions from the Barnahely kennel.

Five generations of Barnahely St Bernards.

which must include at least 4 Major Green Stars, worth five 5 points each. The points awarded depend on the number of dogs shown on the day and can never exceed 10.

The top winning Saint in Ireland is currently the Long-Doyle's Ch Meadowmead Cassandra (page 69 and middle of the top illustration), by Ch Dennis the Menace of Meadowmead out of a daughter of Ch Montaryie Galestorm, winner of the CC at Crufts in 1988. Cassandra won the Annual Champion title awarded by The Irish Kennel Club in 1993 and 1995, and was also awarded the CACIB and BOB at the World Congress in 1995. Cassandra's daughter Ch Longsdyle Dom Perignon (pictured on the left in the top photograph) is the top winning bitch in 1996, gaining her title at just two years of age. She was Best St Bernard Puppy at the World Congress Show in 1995 and holds the trophy for most points won in 1995–1996. The current top winning dog is Mrs Mary Maxwell's Ch Montaryie Juno (pictured on the right in the top illustration), who has won many Green Stars and BOBs.

The Oatfield kennel of Seamus Oates, who judges the breed in Great Britain, is well-known. He and Miss Marjorie Hindes are associates and have campaigned each other's dogs in their respective countries. In 1988 Miss Hindes made up in Great Britain Ch Oatfield Nero, bred by Mr Oates from Ch Burtonswood Be Mighty. Ch Oatfield Nero later became an Irish Champion.

The Barnahely kennels of Mrs Geraldine Barry have achieved much success in both countries. She bought her first St Bernard, 'Beau', as a pet in 1980 and decided to show him. He became Ir Ch Glasslyn Malachite.

Ir Ch Longsdyle Dom Perignon. Top winning bitch in Ireland, 1966. Photo: Long-Doyle.

Ir Ch Glasslyn Malachite.

Twelve other champions have followed, including Ch/Ir Ch Ballincollig and Ch/Ir Ch Ballingeary of Barnahely, both sired by Malachite (see middle photograph on page 70). Geraldine is assisted in her work by husband Kevin and brother-in-law Michael. The kennel had the honour of making up the first Smooth champion bitch to be bred in Ireland, Ch Barnahely Be Beautiful.

Italy

The name Dr Antonio Morsiani is synonymous with Italian St Bernards. Dr Morsiani devoted a lifetime to the breed, and built up his famous Soccorso kennel at the Villa Morsiani, near Bagnara di Romagna. His original aim was to restore size to the breed, and his bloodlines were based on imported stock from Switzerland and

Int Ch Zito del Soccorso, aged 20 months.

Giovanni and Pier Luigi Morsiani with Vincent, Zito, Zeda and Axel del Soccorso.

Germany. One of his most famous dogs was the Swiss import Ch Anton von Hofli, who died in 1969 and was the sire of the great Ch Lorenz von Liebiwil, said to have stood 93cm (36^1/$_2$in) at the shoulder.

Dr Morsiani was assisted in his work by his wife, Marie Leda, and his two sons, Giovanni and Pier Luigi. He wrote extensively about the breed, producing numerous line drawings to

Dr Morsiani judging the United St Bernard Club Championship Show in 1988. Photo: Tony Reed.

illustrate his interpretation of the standard, especially in relation to the planes of the head, about which he was fanatical.

Dr Morsiani judged throughout the world and came to England in 1988 to judge the United St Bernard Club's Diamond Jubilee Championship Show, making Mr George Rudman's Rough dog Topvalley Looking Good Man BIS from a large entry. Shortly before his death from cancer in March 1995, Dr Morsiani judged the German Club's Centennial Show, with over 300 entries.

St Woods Buster, Best Rough in Show, Spanish St Bernard Club Show, 1995.

Spain

When the first edition of this book was published in 1979 St Bernards were almost unknown in Spain. The situation has now changed dramatically; stock has been imported from Europe

St Woods Doc, Best Puppy, 1995.

and Scandinavia and a flourishing Breed Club has come into existence. Admission to the World Union of St Bernard Clubs has been granted.

In 1995 the Club Show at Seville drew entries from 83 Saints, of which 65 were present. Best Rough in Show was St Woods Buster, owned jointly by the Club President, Kari Augestad, and Criadero Estepona. Best Smooth in Show was a dog recently imported from Denmark, St Cardis Walmer, the property of Lise and Jan Stisager. Rafaal Ferreiro won Best Puppy with St Woods Doc, also a Smooth.

Carlos Lopes da Silva's Farah De Sous La Dent.

Winning brace at the Spanish Show, Rambo and Viena de Avin, owned by Vieram de Goltasani.

The Club publishes an extremely good magazine, containing colour pictures of all the top winners and a judge's critique on each dog shown.

Portugal

The St Bernard Club of Portugal was founded in 1996 and is already one of the most active breed clubs in the country. Its President is Carlos Lopes da Silva. There are over 100 members, whose kennels are mainly located in the north of the country. The Club operates from Ermesinde, near Oporto, where it held its first Championship Show in December 1996. Rough Saints outnumber Smooths by about fifteen to one.

France

The breed is not numerically strong in France, although there is a St Bernard Club, affiliated to the World Union, which hosted its show in 1991.

The Benelux Countries

Belgium and Holland are members of the World Union and have acted as hosts to its shows. Owing to their geographical position, their shows are popular with exhibitors from elsewhere in Europe, who have been known to scoop the top awards.

The most noted Belgium breeder from 1920–35 was Madame la Duchesse Douairière de Croy of the Solitude kennel. The breed recovered slowly after World War II and a Club was formed in 1972. Its Club Show in 1996 attracted entries from all over Europe. Best in Show was the Swedish-bred Rough, Int Ch Bernegardens Jackpot. A Belgian-bred Smooth was runner-up.

Doyen of the breed in Holland was the late Albert de la Rie, whose Siegfried kennel was active from 1916 to 1936. His breeding programme was based mainly on Swiss bloodlines. Shortly after the war, Albert de la Rie and his wife moved to Switzerland, where he continued to judge world-wide and support his brainchild, the World Union of St Bernard Clubs. The Dutch St Bernard Club, which was founded in 1926, is one of the most powerful in Europe,

It's a Saint's life for Farah and Emir on the shores of the Atlantic near Oporto, Portugal.

Belgian Rough bitch. Photo: M E Collis.

Int Ch Bernegardens Jackpot. Photo: M E Collis.

Int Ch Bernegarden's Ambassador for Wardana.

being second in numbers only to the German. There is a tendency for Dutch dogs to be smaller and lighter-boned than our British St Bernards, and a number have short muzzles and very pronounced stops. Several Dutch dogs have been imported into Great Britain, but so far appear to have had little significant impact on the development of the breed in this country.

Luxembourg has a small nucleus of keen exhibitors, who support shows elsewhere in Europe and run their own events. Luxembourg is a member of the World Union of St Bernard Clubs. Int Ch Bernegardens Ragtime was Luxembourg's top winner in 1996.

Scandinavia

Britt Halvorsen's Bernegardens are the leading winners in Sweden, and dogs of her breeding have enjoyed marked show success elsewhere in Europe as well as being exported to many countries. A recent export into the United Kingdom is Int/Dutch/Belgium/Lux Ch Bernegardens Ambassador for Wardana, bred in Sweden and sold to a Belgian kennel as a pup. He is all-American on his sire's side and English, German and Dutch on his dam's.

Denmark has produced some notable St Bernards. One winning strain is Karen Neilsen's St Cardis line. Her dogs have been exported to America and to Spain, where they have made useful foundation stock.

A Russian-bred St Bernard, now living in Dubai, cooling off in the Gulf. Photo: Flint.

The Danish St Bernard Club was established in 1973 and is a member of the World Union.

Russia

One of the first dog shows in Russia, organised by Pedigree Petfoods, took place in Moscow in 1992. There were 60 variety classes, in some of which St Bernards competed.

Large dogs are popular in Russia, and their ownership was actively encouraged during the time of the Cold War. At this time a large family might be crowded into a one-room apartment, but owners of giant dogs qualified for a special food allowance and could be rehoused in roomier conditions.

Large dogs known as *Stoistoichenair* are fairly common and are used as guards. They are said to be St Bernard/Mastiff crosses and are smaller than normal Saints, often having docked tails.

Pure-bred St Bernards are produced in Russia, and often find their way to the Middle East, where they may grace the establishments of wealthy oil barons.

Barkley, a Rough Belgian puppy. Photo: M E Collis.

Chapter Five

Becoming a St Bernard Owner

'We've always wanted a St Bernard'

This is said so many times by prospective St Bernard buyers, but all too often the dream fades away once the practical difficulties of coping with such a giant dog are experienced.

The modern Saint is as different from its Alpine ancestors as it is possible to be. It is larger, less athletic, probably rough-coated as opposed to smooth-coated, and differs in head type. This dog can be difficult to control, unless properly trained. You will be taking into your home a massive, strong dog that requires a great deal of care and attention if it is to develop into an animal of which you can be truly proud.

St Bernards are not dogs for the house proud! Photo: M E Collis.

Before committing yourself to providing a caring home for a St Bernard puppy for the rest of its life, it is sensible to ask yourself if you really have the ability and strength to control such a powerful dog. A St Bernard is sufficiently intelligent to 'work out' its owner and, if it finds out that its own will and strength are dominant, there will be problems.

A group of Hartleapwell St Bernards prepare to 'dine out' at Henllys Hall.

St Bernards are sociable animals; they hate to be left alone and are unsuitable pets for families where all members are away for most of the day. A bored and lonely dog may become destructive, and much damage can be done by a frustrated St Bernard. It is sometimes said that you live with St Bernards rather than they with you. They are certainly not dogs for the house-proud. Rough-coated ones moult profusely and, as with any large breed, much mud can be brought into the house in wet weather. Some strains slobber freely.

Keen gardeners will not appreciate the Saintly presence, which may turn the precious plot into a mud bath, and some individuals love to dig but cannot tell the difference between weeds and garden plants. We had one who always unearthed tulip bulbs, and I know of another who buried his owner's purse. In some, a tendency to escape may result in fencing at least two metres high. St Bernards are not recommended where there are small children at the toddling stage, as collisions and accidents can easily occur, however well-meaning the dog.

Keen gardeners may not appreciate the Saintly presence. Photo: Tony Davis.

A St Bernard puppy bought from a reputable kennel may (at the time of writing) cost well over £700, the price reflecting the high cost of stud fees, rearing and veterinary bills. Your puppy will not be cheap to feed, and needs a high quality diet, especially during the growing stage, if it is to become a sound and healthy adult. Once reared, your St Bernard should not be unreasonably expensive to keep, but always be prepared for the heavy expenses that go with the ownership of a giant dog.

'I'll dig there later.' Tristam, eight weeks and one day old. Photo: Pauline Harrison.

Apart from an adequate income, there is one commodity essential to the successful ownership of a St Bernard: spare time to devote to the care of the dog throughout its life. If well trained, a St Bernard will not necessarily be out of place in a smallish home, provided you have the time to give it the limited exercise it needs. The moulting problem can be overcome to some extent by regular grooming, and feeding costs can be reduced if you are prepared to take the time and trouble to prepare cheaper foods.

If you train your St Bernard properly, if necessary by enrolling in dog training classes, you should be the owner of an intelligent, gentle, faithful and obedient companion. Your Saint should be a lover and protector of children, a friend to other animals, a wise guard of you and your property, and a wonderful family dog. It will make you many friends and more than repay the love and care you have lavished upon it.

'Of course, we only want a pet!'

This is said many times by would-be St Bernard purchasers searching for their first puppy and, at the time, it is usually true. Such is their pride in rearing and (hopefully!) training the new member of their family that soon a tremendous sense of achievement has arisen, often fostered by the complimentary remarks of their friends. They may be persuaded to take the puppy to a small local show, where perhaps the standard of competition is not high, and they come away with a prize card. Now they are 'hooked', the dog-showing world has another recruit and The Kennel Club a further potential source of revenue. Even the strong-minded buyer who under no circumstances can be persuaded to exhibit the puppy bought as friend and companion will wish this new member of the family to be a typical and healthy specimen of its breed, so some guidance on what to look for when choosing a Saint puppy is essential.

Choosing a St Bernard puppy

Once you have decided that you are a suitable individual or family to be owned by a St Bernard, the search for the right puppy can begin. You can obtain a list of reputable breeders from The Kennel Club, at 1 Clarges Street, Piccadilly, London W1Y 8AB, and they will also supply the current addresses of the Breed Club secretaries. It is a good plan to attend one of the larger dog shows where there are classes for St Bernards, as this will give the opportunity to meet and talk with breeders and to study their dogs. These shows are advertised in the weekly magazines, *Our Dogs* and *Dog World*.

There are those who, having bought a bitch St Bernard puppy at what seems a high price, imagine that they will make their fortune by breeding and selling a large litter at a similar price. In many cases they mate their bitch to the nearest available dog, often not a show specimen, and find the resultant litter difficult to dispose of. As the unsold puppies get larger, their appetites increase, and very often there are neighbour problems resulting from the playful yapping with which a hungry litter often greets the dawn. In desperation, such litters,

Mrs J Evans' Ch Hartleapwell Magic Moments with her son, Hartleapwell Royal Quest.

Mother Mountside Medway Queen with daughter Timeside Mischief Maker.
Photo: Tony Davis.

or the less attractive members of them, are often sold cheaply to dealers and commercial kennels, who then advertise them for sale at inflated prices. The wise buyer will beware of advertisements offering several different breeds for sale, as such kennels have seldom bred the animals they handle. For a young puppy to pass to its new owner via a middleman constitutes a danger to its health and development. If the foundations of sound rearing have not been laid early in the puppy's life, the leeway is difficult, if not impossible, to make up.

Another recent problem has been the activities of so-called puppy farmers, who treat their bitches as puppy machines, producing litters from these pathetic animals at every season, often under horrendous kennel conditions. The RSPCA have lately succeeded in getting some of these dreadful establishments closed down, but stock is still getting through to dealers.

When visiting kennels always ask to see the mother of any puppies offered, and beware of any kennel where there appears to be a large number of litters available. One well-known establishment is licensed to keep over 20 St Bernard bitches for breeding.

You can assess the status of a breeder by asking if he or she actually bred the puppies for sale, and enquire whether he or she shows the stock with success and how many litters are bred per year. Find out whether the breeder is a member of one of the St Bernard clubs and whether the puppies are Kennel Club registered. If so, papers should be available. Many careful breeders take out puppy insurance that covers the puppy for a time after it goes to its new home, and this is a bonus. You should get an assurance that, should an hereditary problem develop in the puppy, redress will be made.

Always beware of the breeder who pressurises you to buy a puppy without questioning you about your home circumstances and suitability as an owner. If you are told that a St Bernard is a suitable pet to keep in a bed-sitter and will thrive on one tin of 'Woof' per day, make your get-away with haste. If you do purchase a puppy, you should be supplied with a diet sheet and full details of how your new pet has been fed.

Before the search for a suitable puppy begins, you must decide whether you want a Rough or Smooth St Bernard, and whether a dog or a bitch. There are not so many Smooth (or short-haired) St Bernards in Britain as on the continent and in the United States of America, but they have their adherents, and their use is essential in serious breeding programmes. They are less frequently seen in the show ring than the rough-haired variety, perhaps because their short coats cannot hide structural faults. Rough Saints should have coats of medium length, which should never be too thick or curly. Rough puppies look more attractive and cuddlesome, but one must remember that their coats require more attention, and more hair is shed when they moult. Smooths often appear lighter-boned than Roughs, and in some cases can be very 'shelly' looking, but a really good Smooth, showing the correct head type and conformation coupled with the desired height and bone, is a dog that cannot be overlooked.

Father and son: Ch Bernegarden's Buckpasser with an Abbotsbury puppy. Photo: Trevor Goodwin.

The sex of the puppy is a matter of personal preference. If there is no intention of breeding, many families prefer a male animal, to avoid the inconvenience of seasons. Pet females can be spayed, but this is a fairly expensive operation, not without risk, and may result in a tendency to obesity, unless the diet is watched very carefully. It is said females make gentler, more docile pets, but the most gentle-natured St Bernard I have known was a male, and the most tomboyish a bitch, so one cannot generalise. Occasionally some male dogs tend to become rather too amorous and over-sexed, which can prove embarrassing. A fully-grown male St Bernard is heavier and stronger than a bitch so, if the new owner is a woman, the

This Rough puppy grew up to become the top-winning St Bernard of 1995 –
Ch Timeside Mr Sloba-Doba. Photo: Tony Davis.

decision should perhaps be in favour of a bitch. Even in these enlightened days, few of the fair sex have the strength to act as sheet anchor to a 90kg St Bernard intent on setting off in an undesired direction.

Ideally, puppies should go to their new homes at eight weeks old. By this age they should have grown used to life without their mothers without forming close attachments to the people with whom they have contact. Sometimes a breeder may agree to part with a puppy as young as seven weeks, if it is forward and is going to someone who is experienced enough to care for it. Beware of the kennel willing to sell an even younger puppy, as in this case the youngster's welfare cannot be their prime concern.

No-one is infallible when it comes to selecting a puppy; common sense is almost as important as expert knowledge. Choose your puppy very carefully, as you will not be able to change it, as you would your car, for a more attractive model. Never buy on impulse or in a hurry. Do not let your heart rule your head, as the pathetic little runt you feel so sorry for may land you with veterinary fees which will buy the vet a new car.

St Bernard puppies are exceptionally attractive and, as a prospective purchaser, you must not allow yourself to be so carried away with enthusiasm for the appealing youngsters that you lose your critical faculties. Notice whether the puppies and runs are reasonably clean. All puppies soil their pens, but several days' accumulation of excrement is a bad sign, as is any indication of diarrhoea.

Always be honest with a breeder about whether a puppy is being bought solely as a pet or as a prospective show specimen. It is impossible to guarantee at eight weeks that a puppy is a show prospect; the breeder can only pick out which one in a litter is the most promising from a show point of view and, even then, so much will depend on how the puppy is reared. If you tell a breeder you may wish to exhibit your new purchase when it is old enough, you should receive help in picking one of the more suitable members of the litter. If you choose one of the better prospects you must expect to pay a slightly increased price for it. Nothing is more annoying to a breeder than to sell a puppy as a pet, at reduced price, and later to see it damaging the reputation of his or her kennels in the show ring. It is possible for a breeder to place Kennel Club endorsements on a puppy's registration papers so that it cannot be shown and its puppies cannot be registered. If you buy a puppy on the understanding that it is solely a pet, you may expect to find that this has been done. While reading this section, you will find it helpful to refer to the diagram on pages 90–91.

St Bernard puppies should be alert and friendly, but do not automatically dismiss one who appears more interested in sleep than in socialising. It could be resting after a spell of play or an extra-good meal. The puppies should look massive, even at six to eight weeks, when they should weigh about 6.8kg (15lb), but the smaller members of the litter may well grow into sounder adults, so do not necessarily dismiss these in favour of the heavyweights.

Markings are important from a show point of view. Ideally, the St Bernard should have a white muzzle, white blaze up its face, white collar, white chest, and white forelegs, feet and end of tail. Many dogs with variations of these markings win in the ring, so you should not

Bonnington, an example of a quality puppy from Hartleapwell.

dismiss an otherwise pleasing puppy because it lacks the copybook markings. It could make an ideal pet.

The head of a typical puppy should be large in proportion to the body, and the skull should be broad and well-rounded. When gripped between the ears, it should feel wide, in fact wider than the width of the muzzle. The ears should be set fairly high, and their rear base should feel almost muscular, causing the back of the ear to stand away from the head. The stop (angle where the bridge of the muzzle joins the face) should be abrupt and almost a right angle. It is sometimes said that the muzzle should look like a square box on the front of the face, and it should be broad and flat across its bridge. If the correct head properties are absent in a puppy, it will lack them when adult.

Examine the mouth carefully. The upper incisors should overlap the lower. If they are slightly overshot at this age, it is not a bad point, as there should be a scissor bite when the jaw develops and the second teeth come through. An undershot jaw will never improve, and tends to worsen as the puppy grows older. Under some judges it is a handicap in the show ring but, if the puppy is being bought as a pet, it is an imperfection that can be overlooked provided that the youngster does not resemble a Bulldog.

A healthy puppy has a cool, moist nose. Avoid one with sore, watery eyes, appearing half closed. In this case the eyelids could be turned inwards, causing irritation, a condition sometimes found in this breed. Likewise, watch for the puppy with drooping lower eyelids, showing inflamed red haw (membrane in the inside corner of the eye). The colour of the eyes is important if you hope to purchase a show puppy. They should be as dark as possible, a sort of slate grey at this age. If they look blue or sandy-coloured the adult is likely to have yellowish tiger eyes, which are out of character in a St Bernard. The nose and lips should be black.

Beware of the pot-bellied puppy, and check for umbilical hernia, which appears as a small bubble in the centre of the tummy. At eight weeks the puppy should be clear of round worms, having been dosed twice for this as a routine. It is important to check the coat for parasites, especially if the puppy is scratching constantly.

It is important to watch the puppies move around and check that they put their feet down facing straight ahead. Try to pick a puppy with well-angulated hindlegs. There should be no marked turning out of the hindlegs during movement, and the puppy should not appear cow-hocked (see diagram on page 98). It is difficult to assess movement at this age as allowance must be made for general looseness of limb. The front legs should appear thick and well-boned, without weak pasterns (ankles) giving a flat-footed appearance. A puppy that seems to have difficulty in rising to its feet should be regarded with caution.

Even if you are lucky enough or sufficiently clever to locate the perfect St Bernard puppy, it will not grow into a fine specimen of its breed unless you take infinite care in the way you rear it. Too much exercise, rough play or incorrect feeding can ruin the most promising puppy, and all the breeder's knowledge and hard work will then count for nothing. So often, if things go wrong, the dog or the breeder is blamed when the fault may well lie elsewhere.

A promising puppy in Eire: Longsdyle Lanson at eight weeks.

Close versions of the FCI International Standard are now used almost everywhere else in the world. Australia has recently abandoned the British standard in favour of the FCI and New Zealand is in the process of doing so.

The Kennel Club and FCI standards are set out below, with relevant comments, so that the differences in content and emphasis can be appreciated. Refer also to fig 6.1 on page 91.

General appearance
Kennel Club: Well proportioned and of great substance.
FCI: There are two varieties of the St Bernard: Short-haired (smooth-coated) and long-haired (rough-coated). Both varieties are of notable size, and have a balanced, sturdy and muscular body, with imposing head and alert facial expression.

Characteristics
Kennel Club: Distinctly marked, large sized, mountain rescue dog.
FCI: Used as companion, guard and farm dog.

Temperament
Kennel Club: Steady, kindly, intelligent, courageous, trustworthy and benevolent.
FCI: Friendly by nature, calm to lively, watchful.

Head and Skull
Kennel Club: Large, massive, circumference of skull being rather more than double its length. Muzzle short, full in front of the eye and square at nose end. Cheeks flat, great depth from eye to lower jaw. Lips deep but not too pendulous. From nose to stop, perfectly straight and broad. Stop somewhat abrupt and well-defined. Skull broad, slightly rounded at top, with fairly prominent brow. Nose large and black with well developed nostrils.
FCI: Strong, broad, seen in profile and from the front, slightly rounded; sideways it merges gently into the strongly developed high cheek bones, falling away steeply towards the

Fig 6.2: St Bernard heads

The ideal head, showing correct stop; rounded skull; short, deep muzzle; well-rounded flews; small diamond eye; correct ear set.

This dog has a good short muzzle and correctly rounded flews, but its head is spoilt by lack of roundness in top-skull.

This dog has a good round skull, but its muzzle is too long and sloping, and the flews are too cut away.

muzzle. The occipital bone is only moderately pronounced. The supra-orbital ridges are strongly developed. The skin of the forehead forms wrinkles over the eyes which become more pronounced when the dog is attentive. When alert, the set on of the ear and the topline of the skull form a straight line.

The stop is markedly pronounced. The muzzle is short and does not taper. The bridge of the muzzle is flat and its length is shorter than its depth, measured at the root of the muzzle. The edge of the lips should be black. The flews of the upper jaw are strongly developed and pendulous, forming a wide curve towards the nose.

Ch Abbotspass Benedick (1930) showing flat skull, lack of stop, sloping muzzle and cut-away flews.

Comments: The head properties of a St Bernard are so important that, under the old points system (now obsolete), 40% of the total marks were allocated to the head. The skull must be well-rounded from front to back and must look broad and slightly rounded when seen from the front. English dogs before World War II were criticised for flatness of skull, probably a legacy of the Mastiff cross. This has a tendency to make the expression hard and stern.

A clearly-defined stop is of great importance, and should be a true right angle, not a mere slope. Many present-day dogs fail in this respect.

Ths male's face has a 'froggy' appearance, due to the strongly-developed cheek bones. Photo M E Collis.

According to the standards, the domed skull sometimes praised in judges' reports is incorrect. A dome is surely more than slightly rounded and, if the ears are set correctly, the skull should curve gently rather than peaking like St Paul's Cathedral. The comment in The Kennel Club Breed Standard that the circumference of the skull should be more than double its length is meaningless without mention of the points and direction of measurement. The

Ch Whaplode Unique shows correctly-rounded skull, well-set ears with rear edge standing away from head, and expressive diamond eyes.

strongly developed supra-orbital ridges are important, as they prevent the loose skin of the forehead from falling over the eyes and contributing to eye problems.

There is divergence in the two standards concerning the cheeks, The Kennel Club calling for flat cheeks and the FCI for strongly-developed, high cheek bones. In past years these were known as cheek bumps and were considered a fault in Great Britain. When over-developed they can be very ugly, giving a froggy-faced appearance.

Eyes

Kennel Club: Of medium size, neither deep-set nor prominent. Eyelids should be reasonably tight, without any excessive haw. Dark in colour and not staring. There should be no excessive loose wrinkle on brow which would detract from a healthy eye.

FCI: Colour dark brown. Not too deeply set with a friendly expression. Eyelids as close fitting as possible. Complete pigmentation on eye rims. Natural tightness of the lids desired. A small angular wrinkle of the lower eyelid, with slight showing of the haw, as well as a small angular wrinkle of the upper eyelid, are allowed.

Mr D Owen's Smooth bitch, Ch Denbow Miss Muffit, showing correctly-rounded skull and pronounced facial folds.

Comments: There is little difference here. An eye with a small angular wrinkle, as mentioned above, is known as a diamond eye. It is seldom seen today, but its presence in a healthy eye gives the dog a wonderfully sagacious expression. The Kennel Club standard before 1986 called for rather small, deep set eyes, dark in colour, not too close together, the lower eyelid drooping to show a fair amount of haw at the inner corner, the upper eyelid falling well over the eye. This was a recipe for entropion, which was frequent. The profusely-wrinkled skin above the eyes fell forward, its weight causing the upper eyelids to turn in. Poor development of the bony supra-orbital ridge above the eye socket aggravated the problem. Dogs were frequently seen with scars above the eyes, resulting from operations to remove the surplus skin. If untreated, the ingrowing eyelashes could in severe cases irritate the cornea and cause blindness. Ectropic, loose lower eyelids were also fairly common,

resulting in the presence of saucer-shaped areas of red haw below the eyes. These often became infected and inflamed. Today there has been some improvement in the degree of the problem, but weepy eyes are still seen far too often.

There is some confusion about what is meant by a dark eye. If an eye is truly dark, the iris (coloured area around the pupil) should be as dark as the pupil. Today this is seldom seen and light, staring eyes are becoming all too common.

Ears

Kennel Club: Medium size, lying close to the cheeks, not heavily feathered.

The ears of this bitch are set much too low and lack strength in the burr. The skull therefore appears narrow and domed.

FCI: Medium size, set on high and wide; strongly developed burr at base, ear flaps pliable, triangular, and rounded at the tips. The back edge stands off slightly, the front edge lies close fitting to the cheeks.

Comments: All too often the head is ruined by ears that are set too low and lack the essential strong development of the burr (inside structure). When the dog is alert, the ear muscles raise the ears slightly and bring them forward so that they are in line with the top of the skull and, with the burrs standing away, enhance the essential impression of roundness. Flaccid, low-set ears can never do this, and make the skull look too narrow and domed, instead of showing the broad, gentle curve essential to the beauty of the correct St Bernard head.

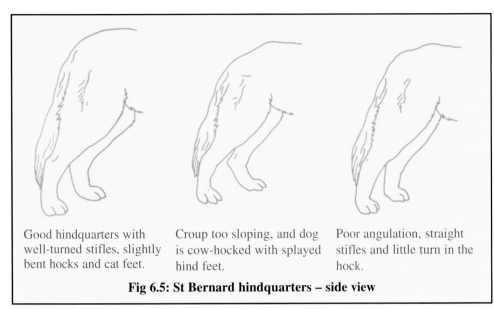

Good hindquarters with well-turned stifles, slightly bent hocks and cat feet.

Croup too sloping, and dog is cow-hocked with splayed hind feet.

Poor angulation, straight stifles and little turn in the hock.

Fig 6.5: St Bernard hindquarters – side view

insufficiently deep or too-narrow chest is also undesirable and gives the dog a shelly appearance and lack of power. If the tail is set on too high there is no downward slope to the croup and the back appears too long. A male St Bernard should be fairly short-coupled, but more length is acceptable in a bitch.

Hindquarters
Kennel Club: Legs heavy in bone, hocks well bent, thighs very muscular.
FCI: The hindquarters should be muscular with moderate angulation. Seen from the rear the hindlegs are parallel and not too close together. The upper thigh is strong and muscular, with broad buttocks. The stifle is well-angulated, turning neither in nor out. The lower thigh is slanting and rather long. The hocks are moderately angulated and strong. The rear pasterns are straight and parallel when seen from behind.

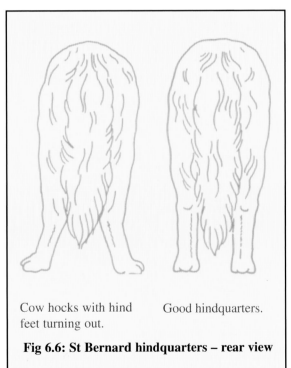

Cow hocks with hind feet turning out.

Good hindquarters.

Fig 6.6: St Bernard hindquarters – rear view

Comments: The hindquarters are most important and should be large with moderately well-turned stifles. The hocks must be set low and only a very slight turning out of the back feet is permissible. Cow hocks and straight stifles are common faults, as are loose hocks, which, owing to a shortness of the calcaneum (heel bone), may result in an almost double-jointed action when the dog moves. Because of the weight of the body, an over-angulated St Bernard is most undesirable.

When a Saint moves, its hocks should not turn in or out, but should move straight forward in a vertical direction. If a dog is straight in stifle, it tends to swing its hocks in an outward direction when moving to gain propulsion. The front feet should clear the ground without dragging, but a high-stepping, hackney action is incorrect. They too should move in a straight vertical plane, neither swinging out like paddles nor crossing inwards and plaiting.

Feet
Kennel Club: Large, compact with well-arched toes. Dewclaws removed.

FCI: Broad and compact, with strong well-arched toes. Dewclaws tolerated as long as they do not hamper movement.

Comments: The feet should be broad and tight, with powerful, strongly-arched toes. They should be cat-like rather than flat, splay-toed or hare-like. Splay feet are a common fault and can sometimes be improved by exercise on hard ground. (See fig 6.4 on page 97.)

Tail
Kennel Club: Set on rather high, long, carried low when in repose; when excited or in motion should not curl over the back.

FCI: Set on broad and strong. Tail long and heavy, its last vertebra reaching at least to the hocks. When in repose, the tail hangs straight down, or may turn gently upwards in its lower third. When animated it is carried higher.

Comments: A tail carried over the back during movement is a common and unsightly fault. The tail is one of the most beautiful features and in Roughs the coat on it should be long and profuse. As explained in the FCI standard, a slight curl in the tail-tip is permissible, but a ring-tail is a very obvious fault, especially in Smooths. If the tail is set too high it tends to be carried gaily (curled over the back when the animal moves).

Movement
Kennel Club: Easy extension, unhurried or smooth, capable of covering difficult terrain.

FCI: Coordinated smooth reaching strides, with good drive from hindquarters. Hindquarters track in line with forequarters.

Coat
Kennel Club: In Roughs, dense and flat, rather fuller round neck, and thighs. Tail well feathered. In Smooths, close and hound-like with slight feathering on thighs and tail.

FCI: In Smooths the coat should be dense, smooth, close-lying and coarse, with rich undercoat. The buttocks should be lightly breeched and the tail covered with dense fur. In Roughs the topcoat is of medium length with a rich undercoat. Over the haunches and the rump it is usually somewhat wavy. The front legs are feathered, the buttocks well-breeched, the hair is short on the face and the tail is bushy.

Colour
Kennel Club: Orange, mahogany-brindle, red-brindle, white with patches on body of any of the above-named colours. Markings as follows: white muzzle, white blaze on face, white collar, white chest, white forelegs, feet and end of tail. Black shadings on face and ears.

FCI: Basic colour white, with either small or large reddish brown patches (splash coat) or a continuous reddish brown jacket covering back and flanks (mantle coat). A torn reddish brown mantle broken up by white is of equal value. Reddish brown brindle permissible, and brownish yellow tolerated. Dark brown shadings on head desirable. Slight black shadings on body tolerated. Markings: chest, feet, tip of tail, muzzle band, and blaze must be white. A white collar and symmetrical dark mask are desirable.

Comments: In this country less attention is paid to markings than overseas. A dog with copy-book markings is less difficult to breed than one of excellent type and conformation. In the 1960s and 1970s dogs with heavy brown or orange ticking (spots) on the white areas of the coat were too often seen in the show ring, and very ugly they looked. Slight dark markings on the white muzzle band are still commonly seen, and would be frowned upon on the continent if too wide-spread.

Size

Kennel Club: Taller the better, provided symmetry is maintained.

FCI:	Minimum height:	Dog	70cm	(27$\frac{1}{2}$in)
		Bitch	65cm	(25$\frac{1}{2}$in)
	Maximum height:	Dog	90cm	(35$\frac{1}{2}$in)
		Bitch	80cm	(31$\frac{1}{2}$in)

Dogs which exceed the maximum height will not be penalised if the general appearance is balanced and the movement correct.

Comments: Point of measurement is not stated; it presumably means at the withers.

Faults

Kennel Club: Any departure from the foregoing points should be considered a fault and the seriousness with which the fault should be regarded should be in exact proportion to its degree.

- Lack of correct gender characteristics
- Unbalanced general appearance
- Muzzle too short or too long
- Excessive wrinkles on head
- Excessive dewlap
- Flews of the lower jaw turning outwards
- Light eyes
- Entropion, ectropion
- Eyelids too loose
- Low set on ears
- Under- or overshot bite
- Missing teeth other than Premolar 1
- Crooked or severely turned out front legs
- Sway or roach back
- Rump higher than withers, or falling away steeply.

- Poorly angulated, bowed, or cow-hocked hindquarters
- Tail carried curled over back
- Faulty movement
- Curly coat
- Incomplete or totally absent pigment on or around nose, on lips and eyelids
- Faulty markings, eg, white with reddish brown ticks
- Faults of temperament: aggressiveness, shyness

Disqualifying faults
- Coat totally white or totally reddish brown
- Coat of an unspecified colour
- Wall eye, blue eye

FCI: Every departure from the foregoing points should be considered a fault which will be assessed according to the degree of departure from the standard.

Note (Kennel Club and FCI): Male animals should have two apparently normal testicles fully descended into the scrotum.

Important proportions specified in FCI Standard

- Ideal proportions for height at withers to body length measured from point of shoulder to point of ischium (pelvis) is 5:6.
- The depth of the chest should ideally be 50% of the total height of the dog measured at the withers.

A St Bernard showing numerous faults: snipey muzzle, too cut away in flews, flat skull, too short in neck, high tail-set, lack of slope in croup, weak pasterns, and straight stifles.

To summarise...

The standards make it abundantly clear that breeders must aim for a massive, powerful, heavily-boned dog with a beautiful expression of intelligent benevolence. Above all, the temperament must match the essential expression, for, if benignity is missing, however closely the dog fits the physical standard, he cannot truly be called a Saint.

Massive does not only mean tall, although this is important. Your true St Bernard is heavily-boned, with powerful muscular shoulders and hindquarters and a large imposing head. It should be emphasised that a massive dog is a powerful dog, and not a fat one!

The minimum heights called for in the FCI standard are exceeded today by most St Bernards in show rings throughout the world, except possibly in the USA, and the proviso in The Kennel Club standard, the taller the better, provided that symmetry is maintained, is an excellent yardstick for judges. Power, type and soundness are of greater importance than height but, if you have these in a dog of imposing stature, you have a truly great St Bernard.

Cornagarth Kuno von Birkenkopf. Photo: Diane Pearce

the union of completely unrelated animals with no common ancestry. The existing St Bernard bloodlines in this country are considerably inbred owing to the numerical limitation of the breeding pool available, so suitable outcrosses are difficult to obtain. To solve this problem, blood from overseas has been introduced on a number of occasions, with varying degrees of success. It has come, for example, from Germany, Switzerland, the United States of America, Holland, and (most recently) from Scandinavia. The results have demonstrated that overseas breeders do not always export their best stock, and breeders obtaining new blood by this method cannot know what lies behind the dogs they have introduced. One most outstandingly successful importation was undoubtedly that of the dog Cornagarth Kuno von Birkenkopf, one of the puppies born in quarantine in this country to a German bitch in 1969. His influence on the breed cannot be over-estimated. He improved soundness, movement and vigour, without obvious sacrifice of type. A similarly successful infusion of new blood could do much for our present-day bloodlines.

Any selected outcross should be as distant as possible, so that the doubling up of recessive faults that may be shared by common ancestors is avoided. Outcrossing always carries inherent risks of introducing new unwanted traits in a strain. The puppies resulting from an outcross mating are usually of assorted type and a breeder will naturally select from them those that resemble his or her preferred type most closely. If they are then bred back to individuals of the breeder's own strain, any benefit of the outcross should become apparent in the second and third generations. Normally, a stud dog resulting from an outcross is less dominant than one more closely bred.

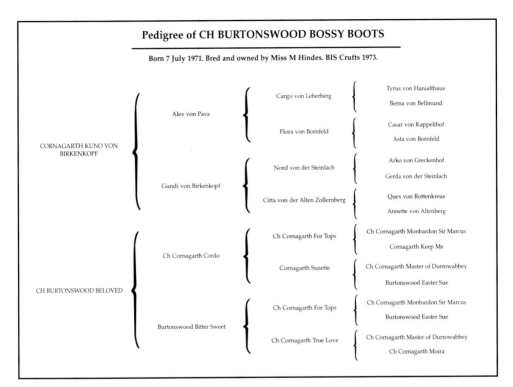

Pedigree of CH BURTONSWOOD BOSSY BOOTS

Born 7 July 1971. Bred and owned by Miss M Hindes. BIS Crufts 1973.

CORNAGARTH KUNO VON BIRKENKOPF	Alex von Pava	Cargo von Leberberg	Tyrus von Hanialthaus
			Berna von Bellmund
		Flora von Bornfeld	Casar von Kappelihof
			Asta von Bornfeld
	Gundi von Birkenkopf	Nord von der Steinlach	Arko von Greckenhof
			Gerda von der Steinlach
		Citta von der Alten Zollernberg	Quex von Rottenkreus
			Annette von Altenberg
CH BURTONSWOOD BELOVED	Ch Cornagarth Cordo	Ch Cornagarth For Tops	Ch Cornagarth Monbardon Sir Marcus
			Cornagarth Keep Me
		Cornagarth Suzette	Ch Cornagarth Master of Durrowabbey
			Burtonswood Easter Sue
	Burtonswood Bitter Sweet	Ch Cornagarth For Tops	Ch Cornagarth Monbardon Sir Marcus
			Burtonswood Easter Sue
		Ch Cornagarth True Love	Ch Cornagarth Master of Durrowabbey
			Ch Cornagarth Moira

Ch Burtonswood Bossy Boots.

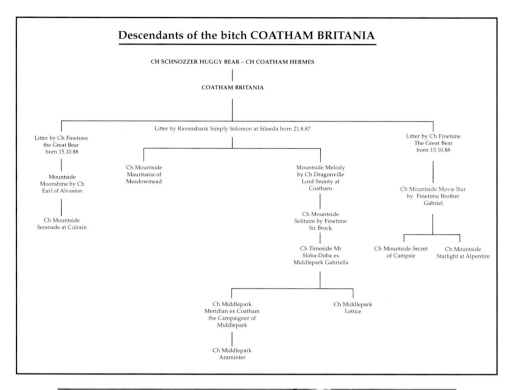

Descendants of the bitch COATHAM BRITANIA

CH SCHNOZZER HUGGY BEAR – CH COATHAM HERMES

COATHAM BRITANIA

Litter by Ch Finetime the Great Bear born 15.10.88

Litter by Ravensbank Simply Solomon at Sileeda born 21.8.87

Litter by Ch Finetime The Great Bear born 15.10.88

Mountside Moonshine by Ch Earl of Alvaston

Ch Mountside Mauritania of Meadowmead

Mountside Melody by Ch Dragonville Lord Snooty at Coatham

Ch Mountside Movie Star by Finetime Brother Gabriel

Ch Mountside Seranade at Culrain

Ch Mountside Solitaire by Finetime Sir Brock

Ch Timeside Mr Sloba-Doba ex Middlepark Gabriella

Ch Mountside Secret of Campsie

Ch Mountside Starlight at Alpentire

Ch Middlepark Meridian ex Coatham the Campaigner of Middlepark

Ch Middlepark Lettice

Ch Middlepark Araminter

Coatham Britania

Breeding Stock, Mating and Whelping

The brood bitch

If you have decided that you have the facilities, time and money to breed your first litter of St Bernards, the choice of a suitable mother is of great importance, especially if you hope to found a successful show kennel. The bitch you intend to use must be of good type, sound, well-balanced, broad in body and, above all, the possessor of a kind and steady temperament. A poor type of bitch is unlikely to breed good puppies, so it is essential to choose a mother without serious hereditary faults. Occasionally, a mediocre bitch can throw a 'flyer', but this can be a disadvantage to the breed, as her descendants in later generations may well inherit her faults. If the bitch from whom you hope to breed does not measure up to these exacting requirements, it may be as well to keep her as a pet and try to buy one more suitable.

Good young breeding bitches are difficult to purchase and, if available, the value of their potential litters renders their cost prohibitive. If you are offered a young bitch who has already been used for breeding, it pays to approach the deal with caution and make careful enquiries about her mothering and whelping capabilities. Do not be tempted to purchase an older bitch who has already had several litters as, after the third litter, the number and quality of a bitch's puppies frequently declines. Sometimes a breeder may sell a bitch on whole or part breeding terms, retaining ownership of some of her future offspring, but arrangements like this can mean you must relinquish the best puppies in the first and sometimes the second litter. If entering into an arrangement of this sort, always make sure that the conditions are clearly set out and signed in a written agreement, as misunderstandings can easily arise.

If you cannot buy a bitch of breeding age, you will have to be more patient and buy a suitable puppy. Try to choose one from a winning strain and a family of good whelpers, and hope that with careful rearing she will make the grade. Many faults obvious in adult St Bernards are not detectable at the puppy stage, but an honest breeder, careful of the reputation of his or her kennel, should help you to select a puppy without obvious imperfections and with show potential. Very short-coupled bitches seldom make good broods; ample length of loin, which may be a handicap in the show ring, is an asset in a breeding animal.

The stud dog

The choice of a suitable stud dog must be made well in advance and needs considerable care and thought. There is an old and true saying that the strength of a kennel lies in its bitches, but the individual dog plays an equally important role.

The need to line up the pedigree of the dog with that of the bitch was explained in the preceding chapter, and it is wise for a novice to line-breed in the first instance, studying the pedigrees of winners from similar bloodlines to those of the mother-to-be. Before making a decision it is most important to study the top winners and their progeny at one of the larger

Whelping Chart

Served Jan	01	02	03	04	05	06	07	08	09	10	11	12	13
Due to whelp Mar/Apr	05	06	07	08	09	10	11	12	13	14	15	16	17
Served Feb	01	02	03	04	05	06	07	08	09	10	11	12	13
Due to whelp Apr/May	05	06	07	08	09	10	11	12	13	14	15	16	17
Served Mar	01	02	03	04	05	06	07	08	09	10	11	12	13
Due to whelp May/Jun	03	04	05	06	07	08	09	10	11	12	13	14	15
Served Apr	01	02	03	04	05	06	07	08	09	10	11	12	13
Due to whelp Jun/Jul	03	04	05	06	07	08	09	10	11	12	13	14	15
Served May	01	02	03	04	05	06	07	08	09	10	11	12	13
Due to whelp Jul/Aug	03	04	05	06	07	08	09	10	11	12	13	14	15
Served Jun	01	02	03	04	05	06	07	08	09	10	11	12	13
Due to whelp Aug/Sep	03	04	05	06	07	08	09	10	11	12	13	14	15
Served Jul	01	02	03	04	05	06	07	08	09	10	11	12	13
Due to whelp Sep/Oct	02	03	04	05	06	07	08	09	10	11	12	13	14
Served Aug	01	02	03	04	05	06	07	08	09	10	11	12	13
Due to whelp Oct/Nov	03	04	05	06	07	08	09	10	11	12	13	14	15
Served Sep	01	02	03	04	05	06	07	08	09	10	11	12	13
Due to whelp Nov/Dec	03	04	05	06	07	08	09	10	11	12	13	14	15
Served Oct	01	02	03	04	05	06	07	08	09	10	11	12	13
Due to whelp Dec/Jan	03	04	05	06	07	08	09	10	11	12	13	14	15
Served Nov	01	02	03	04	05	06	07	08	09	10	11	12	13
Due to whelp Jan/Feb	03	04	05	06	07	08	09	10	11	12	13	14	15
Served Dec	01	02	03	04	05	06	07	08	09	10	11	12	13
Due to whelp Feb/Mar	02	03	04	05	06	07	08	09	10	11	12	13	14

14	15	16	17	18	19	20	21	22	23	24	25	26	27	28	29	30	31
18	19	20	21	22	23	24	25	26	27	28	29	30	31	01	02	03	04
14	15	16	17	18	19	20	21	22	23	24	25	26	27	28	(29)		
18	19	20	21	22	23	24	25	26	27	28	29	30	01	02	(03)		
14	15	16	17	18	19	20	21	22	23	24	25	26	27	28	29	30	31
16	17	18	19	20	21	22	23	24	25	26	27	28	29	30	31	01	02
14	15	16	17	18	19	20	21	22	23	24	25	26	27	28	29	30	
16	17	18	19	20	21	22	23	24	25	26	27	28	29	30	01	02	
14	15	16	17	18	19	20	21	22	23	24	25	26	27	28	29	30	31
16	17	18	19	20	21	22	23	24	25	26	27	28	29	30	31	01	02
14	15	16	17	18	19	20	21	22	23	24	25	26	27	28	29	30	
16	17	18	19	20	21	22	23	24	25	26	27	28	29	30	31	01	
14	15	16	17	18	19	20	21	22	23	24	25	26	27	28	29	30	31
15	16	17	18	19	20	21	22	23	24	25	26	27	28	29	30	01	02
14	15	16	17	18	19	20	21	22	23	24	25	26	27	28	29	30	31
16	17	18	19	20	21	22	23	24	25	26	27	28	29	30	31	01	02
14	15	16	17	18	19	20	21	22	23	24	25	26	27	28	29	30	
16	17	18	19	20	21	22	23	24	25	26	27	28	29	30	01	02	
14	15	16	17	18	19	20	21	22	23	24	25	26	27	28	29	30	31
16	17	18	19	20	21	22	23	24	25	26	27	28	29	30	31	01	02
14	15	16	17	18	19	20	21	22	23	24	25	26	27	28	29	30	
16	17	18	19	20	21	22	23	24	25	26	27	28	29	30	31	01	
14	15	16	17	18	19	20	21	22	23	24	25	26	27	28	29	30	31
15	16	17	18	19	20	21	22	23	24	25	26	27	28	01	02	03	04

Kind of milk	Water	Total Solids	Protein	Fat	Carbohydrates	Other Solids
Bitch	75.4	24.6	11.2	9.6	3.1	0.7
Cow	87.2	12.8	3.5	3.7	4.9	0.7
Goat	85.7	14.3	4.3	4.8	4.4	0.8

Table 9.1: Comparison of various milks

If goat's milk is available, it is excellent for weaning purposes, as it is easily digested. A frozen supply can usually be purchased. Once weaned, the litter can progress to powdered Gold Top Calf Milk or Lamb Milk, mixed at 50% above the recommended strength. Owing to the low carbohydrate content of bitch's milk, it is not advisable to add glucose to the weaning milk, as this increases the sugar content too much. If one must sweeten the milk, honey is a better additive, as it is rich in vitamins.

As the gradual weaning process continues, the bitch should be kept away from her puppies for longer and more frequent intervals and their new meals should become more numerous. By the age of four or five weeks they should be having four daily feeds: two of minced raw meat and two of milk. At this stage, raw egg yolk and a few drops of cod liver oil can be added to the meat feeds and the milk feeds can include baby cereals such as Farex and Farlene. As these cereals are rich in calcium and other minerals, while they are being given other mineral additives should be unnecessary. A good puppy biscuit can be introduced gradually, mixed into the meat. Minced tripe, if available, is a good replacement for meat.

Bitch puppy six weeks, weighing 5.4kg (12lb)

Rearing a

Most careful breeders do
weeks old, by which age tl
the great day for collect
precautions should be tak
pools made inaccessible. In
  It is sensible to restrict t
corner, perhaps in the kitc
confine the puppy to any f
your pup from climbing ou
Lindenhall High Hopes wh
  Stocks of food for the
breeder for advice about wl
with the local butcher, if yo
the puppy and asked not
hours beforehand, to g
sickness. Travelling by
frightening experience for a
wise to travel with a
newspapers, in case of eme
  The move to a new hon
in a puppy's life; not only v
the companionship of its l
have new experiences to fa
meet. Your new puppy will
for the first few hours, whil
new owners and getting ac
surroundings. When its c
established, it will soon co
and play.

Trainin
A poorly-trained dog of
discredit on its owner, and
Bernard is a menace. Unsou
be inherited, but neurotic d
the fault of excitable and err
usually judge the temperam

Ready for the 'off': Gabriella Lee with Gold (14.3kg)
and Bridget (13.21kg) at eight weeks.

At the last stage of weaning,
it is advisable to allow the bitch to
sleep with her puppies and be
separated from them for the rest of
the 24 hours. They then have the
comfort of the natural milk bar
during the long night interval. It is
a good plan to have the puppies
completely weaned by six or seven
weeks, so that they have ample
time to adjust themselves to the
complete absence of their mother
before they leave for their new
homes at eight weeks.

Worming
Many puppies harbour a few
roundworms, although St Bernards
do not seem to become as badly
infested as some of the more low-
to-ground breeds. The sooner these
worms are eliminated the better,
and the first treatment can take
place after three weeks. The use of
Coopane tablets, obtainable from a
vet, is recommended, as the
puppies never suffer any ill-effects
from these. After the first dosing
they usually seem to make
increasingly rapid progress, even if no worms have been seen. The puppies should be
wormed again at six weeks, and once more two weeks later if worms have been passed.

Roughs and Smooths
If one of the parents is smooth-coated, it is likely that the litter will contain puppies of both
coat types, but which are which will not be obvious for about six weeks. The difference is
usually first apparent on the underside of the tail and on the backs of the thighs. In Rough
puppies, these soon begin to fluff up and appear bushy, but tend to remain flat in Smooths.

Puppy progress
To assist novice breeders, who often wonder if the rate of their puppies' development is up
to standard, a dog and a bitch puppy from a recent litter of 11 puppies out of Mr and Mrs
Raby's bitch, Leontonix Sweetheart, were weighed and photographed at weekly intervals.
The weight chart shows that the dog, Leontonix Gold, always slightly outstripped the bitch,
Leontonix Our Bridget, in weight, and both made the most rapid gains between four and
seven weeks, at the time of weaning and worming. All the photographs of Gold and Bridget
were taken by Derek Lee.

potential buyers; you c
owners seem suitable, t
St Bernard ownership.
only too keen to learn.
agrees to return it to yo
can then find a suitable

When a puppy lea
carefully how it should
the puppy's usual food
diet and environment. A
down, and offer to give
puppy should also take
have been received in ti
safeguard the breeder sl

Application for puppy r
form, which must be si
registration number. Al
same form, and this mu
registration on this form

It is possible for the
dog's records, and fo
endorsement can only b
both of the following:
a   Progeny not eligible
b   Not eligible for issue

If you are selling a p
new owner aware of the

It is possible for a br
is a special and exclusiv
changing the name of a
continues to pay for the
£15 annually to maintair

A breeder may place
Therefore, if your affix
possible to change a dog
of another registered ow
become Swisscottage Ja
owner.

Before a registered do
Club into the name of
appropriate Transfer For

Championship shows

These are the classic events of the show world. They may be either All Breed events, with separate classes for a number of different breeds, or Breed events, usually organised by a specialist Breed Club and confined to one particular breed. The most famous championship show is Crufts, now held at the National Exhibition Centre near Birmingham, and managed by The Kennel Club. The larger championship shows are almost invariably benched, and entries must be made up to six weeks in advance. Fees for these shows increase annually, with additional high charges for car parking and catalogues. In past years, it was usual for the winners to receive prize money, but this is no longer the case, although winners at the smaller breed club shows are usually rewarded with trophies and rosettes.

Only at championship shows can dogs win the coveted CCs, of which three must be gained under three different judges to earn the title of Champion. They are awarded to the Best Dog and Best Bitch in most of the classified breeds. To make your dog a champion you may have to travel the length and breadth of the country to collect the three awards required.

Age to show

Puppies under six months old are not eligible for exhibition at any show held under Kennel Club rules. In any case, St Bernard puppies are not mature enough to be taken to shows at this age. If you have a promising puppy, it is better to wait until it is almost a year old before showing it; your dog will be much improved when it has muscled up and matured. Many good puppies have had their development hampered by being dragged from show to show at a tender age when they would have been better left to mature at home in peace and quiet.

Entering for shows

Details of forthcoming shows are published weekly in the advertisement pages of the canine magazines, *Our Dogs* and *Dog World*, together with addresses from which schedules and entry forms can be obtained. Before completing an entry form you should study the definitions of the various classes carefully as, if you enter the wrong class, you will be disqualified later. At some shows a Special Beginners or Special Newcomers class is scheduled to give newcomers a chance, but the definition should be checked carefully as it varies from show to show. If you are entering a young dog it is sensible to enter only in the lower classes rather than be too ambitious. One or two classes are sufficient for a dog's first appearance; a youngster so easily becomes bored standing in the ring for a long period, and this may prejudice that dog against showing at the start of its career.

Show grooming and training

A dog show is a beauty contest and, to stand any chance in keen competition, it is essential that your exhibit is looking its best and trained to show its good points to advantage. The dog should be groomed regularly during the period before the show to stimulate the circulation and improve the condition of its coat. If necessary, it should be bathed all over on the day before the show, or have its tail, legs, chest and underparts washed thoroughly. Too much washing can make a coat 'blow', especially if the dog is nearing the moult. Its ears should be cleaned, and any unsightly loose hair plucked (but never cut) from the outside of the ear flaps and between the toes. If the dog has been well groomed during the preceding weeks there should be no matts in the coat, but it is wise to check the long hair on the thighs, tail and behind the ears. Nails should not need trimming if the dog has had adequate exercise.

Your dog's show training can begin when it is only a puppy. It is most important that the person who will handle your dog in the ring has it under complete control. If it misbehaves and upsets other exhibits, their owners will not be pleased; neither will your chances of being among the winners be enhanced. It should be emphasised that no bad-tempered dog should be taken anywhere near a show. Should the dog bite the judge, another exhibitor or a fellow exhibit, serious injury may result, and you may be reported to The Kennel Club which would probably ban the dog from future shows. At a benched show, spectators, especially children, always fall in love with the St Bernards and try to stroke them, so to take a dog of uncertain temperament to a show is just asking for trouble.

If you have trained your dog well as a puppy, it should be used to walking on a lead without pulling but, before showing your dog, get it used to walking on a loose lead at an easy pace. You must also train it to stand sideways for several minutes without moving, as it will need to do during the judge's assessment. Your dog should be accustomed to having its lips gently lifted to reveal its bite, so that it does not protest when the judge checks this important point. If, before entering a show, you can manage to attend one as a spectator, you will learn much about the routine and understand what is expected of the dogs.

Before setting off for the show you will need to assemble much equipment for yourself and the dog. In addition to the collar and lead you intend to use in the ring, you will need a strong chain to fasten your exhibit to the bench and a rug for it to lie on. Some show benches are horribly grubby, so you may decide to take some mild disinfectant and a cloth along with you as well. For an all-day event you will need a drinking bowl, some food for yourself, and a favourite meal for the dog – who will have earned it before the day is out! Do not forget the grooming equipment and some powder to clean your dog's legs and underparts in case they get wet and muddy. Under Kennel Club rules, all cleaning powder must be removed from the coat before the dog is taken into the ring. A large, clean towel is always useful. If the dog shows any tendency to car-sickness, do not forget the Sea Leg tablets, and you may need a good supply of headache pills for yourself.

Show day

It is wise to set out for the show in good time to allow for the numerous road hold-ups that seem to beset the motorist today. When reaching the show ground you must find a handy parking space for the car, and possibly set out on a 15-minute hike to reach the correct tent and find the right bench for your dog. Nothing is worse than trying to struggle through a large crowded show ground, controlling your St Bernard and carrying all the aforementioned gear, when you know you are late and your class is due to enter the ring. Almost equally harassing is trying to find the money to buy a show catalogue when you are clutching dog and gear.

Benches for St Bernards are sometimes too small and unsteady for the size and weight of the dog, so an unseasoned exhibit may object to the confinement and try to escape. It pays to be very careful and try not to leave your dog alone until you are sure it has settled and grown accustomed to its surroundings. Some modern benches are flush with the ground, which is safer for the dog but leaves the exhibitor with nowhere to sit. A small picnic chair may then be a necessary addition to the show gear.

It is important to find out as soon as possible when your class is likely to be judged; if it is one of the later ones, which it will be if you are showing a bitch, delay your final grooming of the dog until you are almost due to go into the ring. If the weather is hot and the dog tends

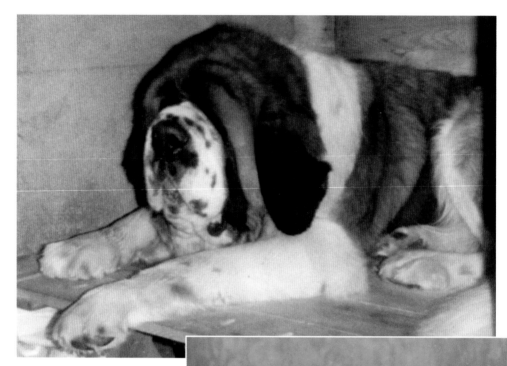

Show dogs resting in their pens. The Champion bitch above has no room to stretch out, and the dog on the right is lying across a gap in the floor.
Photos: Cooper and Raby.

to drool, tie a bib or towel round the neck to keep the dewlap dry.

When your class is called, take the dog into the ring, collect your ring number from the steward and pin it to your person with a ring-clip. Always be calm and confident, even though your knees may be knocking. Dogs soon sense any tenseness on the part of their handlers and may be unsettled in consequence. If you are showing for the first time it is wise to place yourself well along the line of waiting exhibitors, so that you can copy the procedure of those more experienced. While waiting in the ring never allow your dog to interfere with that of another exhibitor.

Judging procedure

Many judges ask all the exhibitors in a class to go round the ring together in a circle before examining the dogs individually. This gives the dogs a chance to settle down and the judge an opportunity for a quick overall survey. He or she will then call each exhibit in turn and examine it thoroughly (or not so thoroughly). The handler will then be asked to move it either in a straight line or in a triangle. It is so important to concentrate all your attention on your dog, and listen carefully to the judge's questions and instructions. The judge will probably ask the age of the dog; if so, you should volunteer simply this information, and not launch into a description of its whole life story or the prizes it won last week at Blanktown Exemption Show. The judge may ask you to move the dog in such a way that he or she can observe its movement from the side, and in this case you must be sure not to place yourself between dog and judge – however good your own movement may be!

Once the judge has completed the appraisal, you should take your place again in the line, or stand where the steward tells you, while the rest of the dogs are examined. Once all have been seen, most judges come down the line again, making a final comparison of the exhibits,

Three Junior Warrant winners from the same litter. Left to right: Burnswark Samantha at Birkenbush with owner Mary Reid; Burnswark Senator of Wyandra, owned by Barbara Swaine-Williams; Burnswark Louisa with breeder Ann Druce. Photo: B Swaine-Williams.

and this is the moment when you must have your dog standing sideways on to the judge, and looking its absolute best. See that it is standing squarely on all four legs with its head held slightly up, but don't fiddle with it too much as this can draw attention to the faults you are trying to hide. Some practised exhibitors 'string up' their dogs at this point, by moving the collar up tightly behind the ears and stretching the head and neck upwards, which makes the back appear shorter and improves the ear carriage. If you have not tried this, it is best not to attempt it for the first time in the ring, as you may unsettle your dog.

If you concentrate on your dog and the instructions of the judge, you will forget to feel nervous and be ready to obey any final request. You may be asked to move your dog again, if the judge wishes to compare its movement with that of another. There is an old adage among judges: When in doubt – move them about, so always be on the alert to obey any instruction promptly.

When the assessment is completed the judge will beckon the winners, or those from whom the winners will be selected, into the centre of the ring. If you are one of the lucky ones, move at once to the position indicated. Never relax until the judging book has been marked, in case the judge changes his or her mind at the last moment.

At the end of the class, always make a fuss of your dog, so that it learns to regard a show as a happy occasion. Always try to accept defeat with a good grace. There will always be another show – and another judge!

If a dog wins its class and is not beaten in a subsequent class, it will be required to enter the ring again, to compete with other unbeaten exhibits for the Best of Sex award which, at a Championship Show will be a Challenge Certificate. The two CC winners then compete for the Best of Breed award. At the end of an all-breed show, the winning St Bernard must meet the other BOB winners among the Working breeds to determine the best in the Working Group. This winner then challenges the winners of the other groups (Terrier, Gundog, Utility, Hound and Toy) for the coveted Best in Show award. To achieve this at a big championship show is every exhibitor's dream, but is an ambition realised by only a few.

Junior Warrants are diplomas awarded by The Kennel Club to winning dogs from 12–18 months old. First prize winners in this age group in Breed classes at championship shows score 3 points, and at open shows 1 point. If a total of 25 points is amassed, a Junior Warrant is awarded.

Once the judging is over, you should return your dog to its bench, and give it a drink and possibly food. Your dog should then settle down and rest until it is time to leave for home. Most of the big shows used to have a strictly enforced removal time, which often meant chaos in the car parks when all the exhibitors tried to leave simultaneously. This is now more flexible, although still enforced at some shows, including Crufts, where the public pay high admission fees to see the dogs. If you have to wait about, this is the time to get acquainted with other exhibitors, who may then have time to talk and answer your questions. Some judges, if they have confidence in their assessment, go round the benches afterwards, so that you have a chance to ask their opinion of your dog. It is customary for every judge to write a report on his or her winners for publication in the dog press, but lately this courtesy is rarely observed by St Bernard judges in this country.

The Kennel Club Stud Book

This massive tome is published annually by The Kennel Club and lists the top show winners of all the various breeds, together with details of their immediate pedigrees. A Stud Book number is allocated to each dog eligible for inclusion. Criteria for entry varies from breed to breed, according to numerical strength. In St Bernards, dogs must win First, Second or Third in Open Classes at shows where CCs are on offer to the breed.

Expert handling: Mrs Joy Evans sets up Ch Hartleapwell Must Be Magic for the judge's inspection.

Judging

At one time it was usual to serve an apprenticeship of several years as a breeder and exhibitor before being invited to judge St Bernards. Recently this has not always been the case as, owing to an increase in the number of shows scheduling the breed, there appeared to be a shortage of specialist judges. The Kennel Club's recent cut in the number of CCs available may do something to redress the balance. During the 'boom' years it was not uncommon to

St Bernard Breed Clubs

Since St Bernards first became popular in the 19th century many organisations have been established to promote the breed, both in this country and overseas.

Bayard and Barry, from a painting in *Cassell's Illustrated Book of the Dog*.

The St Bernard Club

The English breeders were the first to form such a society, and fanciers led by the Rev Arthur Carter did so at a meeting held on 2 February 1882. Almost immediately there was dissension among members but, according to Hugh Dalziel, *it was better for the body as a whole, that the rotten leprous member be cut off, so the disagreeable difficulty was obviated, and the Club has ever since gone on – not... like a house on fire, but like a mansion intended for a common good.*

The pattern of dissension within and between St Bernard Clubs unfortunately has not been uncommon during succeeding years. According to Albert de la Rie, the Swiss Kennel Club was formed in 1883 to protect the St Bernard and with the fear that the British, who in 1882 had already formed a St Bernard Club of their own, would dominate in determining the future type of the Swiss St Bernard dog.

In 1886 both the British and Swiss Clubs drew up standards for the breed, but they could not agree a common theme. In June 1887, a conference was held in Zurich, and the Swiss standard was accepted by representatives of all nations but Great Britain. Since that time the British have followed their own standard. The version drawn up by The Kennel Club in 1986, without consultation with breeders, meant even greater disparity between our standard and that followed almost everywhere else in the world.

Writing in the year book of The St Bernard Club in 1913, its President, L C R Norris-Elye, gives an informative account of its early

Rev Arthur Carter's Smooth bitch Thisbe, exhibited at the St Bernard Club Show in 1885.

years and first shows. He reports that the Duke of Wellington was one of its early patrons, and lent his riding school at Knightsbridge for its first three shows. The carelessness of workmen leaving nails after the benches were removed, thus endangering the horses that used the riding school, led to the building being refused for future shows, so the Club shows were held in different places and sometimes in connection with other shows.

The first show, in 1882, drew 252 entries, and was judged by Rev Cumming MacDona, who exhibited (not for competition) two of his own dogs. The next year's show drew 264 entries, the judges being Rev Arthur Carter and Mr S W Smith. The third show had 247 entries, and here the great Plinlimmon made his appearance, together with the noted bitch, Thisbe. In June of the following year, the show moved to Southport and the entry fell to 170. Plinlimmon's dam, Bessie II, was among the winners. A further show was held in December 1886 at the Albert Palace, Battersea, and drew a slightly increased entry. Another event was held in 1887 at Lillie Bridge. Sheffield was the venue for the Club's eighth show, also in 1887. It drew 217 entries, including Sir Bedivere (see overleaf), Keeper and Watch.

The ninth show, in 1889, took place at Windsor in conjunction with The Royal. The route to The Royal was changed at the last moment, so the crowd, instead of passing the entrance to the St Bernard show, was diverted to another road, ruining the Club's gate money and injuring tradesmen who had rented plots on the original route. This was the first Club Show

Beldene Saints at Queensbury, near Leeds. Mr A K Gaunt was secretary from 1947 until 1974. The Club's first Championship Show was held near Nottingham in 1979 with Mr M Whitelaw choosing Ch Burtonswood Black Tarquin as BIS.

Others

Two regional Clubs for the benefit of exhibitors in the Eastern and Southern Counties have been set up since 1984. The Eastern St Bernard Society held its first championship show in 1989, when Hartleapwell Midnite Magic was BIS under Mr J Harpham.

The Eastern Club Show, 1992. Judge Mrs Deuchar Fawcett with
(left) Barbara Swaine-Williams with Ch Coatham Good News for Wyandra (BIS) and
(right) Judy McMurray with Ch Mountside Starlight at Alpentire (Best Opposite Sex).

The St Bernard Trust

Whether as the result of over-breeding or the difficult economic situation currently existing in this country, the problem of unwanted St Bernards grows ever more worrying. To cope with the situation, the United St Bernard Club set up a Trust in 1988, which is registered with the Charity Commission (No. 328192), and has received support from other clubs. Its work of rehoming unwanted St Bernards is financed entirely by voluntary donations. Fund-raising

This bitch was found wandering the country lanes of Pembrokeshire.

Methy, who came to the Trust with a badly-set broken leg.

efforts include raffles, stalls at shows, tombolas, exemption shows, street collections, and many other enterprises. When films about a St Bernard called Beethoven were recently screened in this country, Trust supporters even stood outside cinemas and rattled their collecting tins.

The Trust has to find new homes for between 60 and 80 St Bernards annually. Some are picked up off the streets, often in bad physical shape. Others are passed to the Trust for a variety of genuine reasons, and less genuine excuses. Often the unfortunate animals have been purchased from puppy farms and backyard breeders, who fail to check if their customers are able to cope with giant dogs, and give no guidance whatever about rearing and training. Many of the dogs reaching the Trust have behaviour problems and are therefore difficult to re-home. Reasons for 'the St Bernard must

go' syndrome include family break-up, owners out at work all day, unemployment, moving house, new baby, dog aggressive, neighbour problems, dog too lively for children, and children allergic to dog hair. In many cases one wonders why the dog was bought in the first place.

All prospective homes are visited by representatives of the Trust to check their suitability. The Trust does not sell dogs, but donations are requested from new owners.

Young Smooth dog, found tied to a lamp-post.

often eases the breathing by dilating the bronchial tubes. Overweight Saints are more prone to bronchial problems so, if your dog suffers, reduce its weight.

Disorders of bones and joints

Sprains

Because of their weight, St Bernards are especially prone to injuries of joints, tendons and ligaments. In the case of puppies, awkward falls during exercise and play can result in injuries that only rest and time will cure. A simple muscle sprain may benefit from the application of ice-cold compresses.

Torn ligaments are a much more serious matter, and damage to the cruciate ligament in the hind leg is a common problem in St Bernards, causing severe lameness that can only be rectified by operative treatment. After surgical repair of the ligament, a prolonged period of rest and recuperation is necessary, until complete healing of the injury has taken place.

Arthritis

This often affects the joints of older dogs and is especially common in those with poor hip structure. Friction within a dysplastic joint (see below) can lead to undue wear on the articular surfaces of the bones, causing pain in later life. Sufferers should be kept warm and dry and treatment with anti-inflammatory drugs may give some relief.

Hip Dysplasia (HD)

Many of the larger breeds of dogs are prone to this malformation of the hip joint, among those worst affected being Clumber Spaniels, Newfoundlands, Bullmastiffs and Old English Sheepdogs. The reasons for its incidence are not fully understood, but hereditary factors almost certainly play a part. In the correct hip joint, the acetabulum (socket on the pelvis) is a deep, rounded hollow into which the head of the femur (ball) fits closely. In the dysplastic joint, the socket may be shallow and the femoral head flattened instead of rounded. The ball is thus incompletely engaged in the socket and, when it is palpated, the joint feels loose and badly connected. The ligaments attached to the joint may be slack or torn and, as already explained, arthritis is likely to set in as the dog ages, owing to undue wear of the articular surfaces.

Hip Dysplasia (HD) is investigated by X-ray and varies from mild cases, where there is a poor fit between the ball and the socket, to very severe manifestations, where the socket is totally flattened and the head of the femur is completely displaced. Mild cases usually improve, as the muscles develop and hold the joint in place. Many growing St Bernards exhibit looseness of gait and apparent stiffness in the hind limbs, and a number of vets grow rich by alarming owners about the severity of slight abnormalities in the hip joint.

The British Veterinary Association and The Kennel Club have a hip scoring scheme. Their aim is to X-ray and score as many individuals within a breed as possible so that average data for that breed can be calculated. Each hip is scored separately and marks out of 6 are awarded on nine different aspects of the structure, giving a possible total of 54 for each side. A high score indicates a deformed hip, the worst possible combined total being 108. A recent average for St Bernards was 20:17.

Only a small percentage of breeders are willing to submit their dogs for testing, as many St Bernards react badly to anaesthesia, which is necessary when the X-ray photographs are taken. What is certain is that progress in eliminating this distressing condition will not be made while dogs with high hip scores continue to be used for breeding and judges, both specialists and all-rounders, continue to condone unsound hind movement.

There are several ways of treating a dysplastic dog. Drugs may be used to ease pain, or it may be advisable to resort to surgery. The cutting of the pectinous muscle in the groin can reduce the pull on the joint, or the head of the femur may be removed completely to eliminate friction and pain. It is suggested that when HD is treated in this way to disguise defects, the dog should be castrated or spayed so that it cannot be bred from.

Research has shown a correlation between the weight of the muscle-mass surrounding the hip joint and the incidence of dysplasia. Greyhounds, who never exhibit dysplasia, have been shown to have a higher pelvic muscle-mass in proportion to their total body weight than other breeds, and this applies even if the animals have not been trained for racing. Treatment to build up the muscle-mass with drugs has been tried with some success, Vitamin E having long been known to assist muscular development. It has also been shown that the puppies who gain the most weight during the first few months of life are the most likely to have poor hip structure, while puppies who gain weight slowly and regularly are less at risk.

Osteochondrosis

This problem, occurring in St Bernards and other large breeds, affects the cartilage of the joints in shoulder, elbow, hock and stifle. It is most common in puppies of three to eight months. It is caused by a delay in the conversion of cartilage to bone in the growth plates, which are found at the ends of the long bones. Cartilage is made up of a series of layers of gelatinous tissue, which do not contain blood vessels and are nourished by the synovial fluid from the joints. When the layers are abnormally thick, trouble may occur in the deeper ones and some may start to break up and split off. The resultant cavity then fills with synovial fluid, causing inflammation followed by arthritis.

If part of the cartilage actually separates from the joint, the condition is known as Osteochondrosis Dissecans (OCD) and the loose fragments may continue to grow and cause great trouble. The detached cartilage can be removed surgically, and diseased material can be scraped away from the joint surface. In some cases the fragments may even be reabsorbed and the lameness can disappear, but arthritis may eventually set in.

Male dogs are more often affected than females, as they tend to be heavier and more boisterous. It is not uncommon for several litter mates to show symptoms of OCD, and breeding from affected stock is most unwise, as the disease may be genetically linked. Giving excess calcium and adding various mineral and vitamin supplements haphazardly to the diet are not recommended. Sterilised boneflour and nutritionally-balanced puppy foods are safer ways of getting the right mineral balance.

Swollen elbow

This is caused by an accumulation of fluid within the elbow joint and is similar to the athlete's water on the knee. It is caused by the dog throwing its full weight on a hard surface when lying down, damaging the fluid capsule within the joint. Heavier St Bernards are more prone to this condition, which is likely to occur when the kennel flooring is concrete or stone rather than wood. A successful treatment in the past was Iodex ointment, applied every other day until the condition cleared up, but this preparation is now difficult to obtain.

Operative treatment under sterile conditions may be combined with the instillation of long acting steroids such as Depomedrone. It may be necessary to repeat the treatment again

Mastitis

This inflammation of the milk glands is usually the result of a bitch having too much milk, either because her puppies have been removed or because the demands of her litter are too small. It can occur in one or more glands as a result of injury, or blockage of a teat from which the puppies will not suck. Abscesses may form in the glands, and soreness and swelling occur. The trouble may be treated with antibiotics squeezed into the teat and by drugs to reduce the milk flow.

Metritis

Inflammation of the womb may occur after the birth of puppies, and can be the result of the presence of a dead puppy or retained afterbirth. Less serious cases usually respond to antibiotics.

Pyometra

Like metritis, the symptoms of pyometra (pus in the womb) are distension of the abdomen and a foul-smelling, dark brown discharge. There is often vomiting and excessive thirst. The condition is more common in older bitches and, in most cases, hysterectomy (removal of the womb) is necessary. If pyometra is suspected, treatment should be prompt. The operation is usually successful if done in time, and many bitches take on a new lease of life after it has been carried out. There may, however, be a tendency to put on weight afterwards, so food intake may have to be controlled.

False pregnancy

Whether a bitch has been mated or not, she can sometimes show all the signs of being in whelp when she is not. There may be abdominal swelling, production of milk, and all the other signs of approaching labour, such as panting and bed-making. If the condition is severe, it may be necessary to give sedatives and tablets to reduce the milk flow, but usually the symptoms clear up naturally within a few days. Bitches in this state can make ideal foster mothers. If there is a history of false pregnancies after each season, the bitch may eventually have to be spayed.

Disorders of male dogs

Monorchidism

In this condition a dog has only one testicle descended into the scrotum. Another may be present but retained within the body cavity. It is a disqualifying fault in the FCI standard. Monorchids are capable of siring puppies, but should not be used at stud, as the condition is hereditary. A monorchid may sire cryptorchid offspring.

Cryptorchidism

Cryptorchids have no testicles within the scrotum and are sterile.

Disorders due to parasites

Like all dogs, the St Bernard may play host to a variety of internal and external parasites. The mites which can cause skin, foot and ear problems have already been mentioned. Owners must be continually on the look-out for such infestation as, owing to the size of the St Bernard, eradication once parasites are established can be a major problem. Various species of worm may live inside the body, and parasitic insects can live on its surface, causing varying degrees of unthriftiness and ill-health.

Roundworms

These can vary in length from 2.5–20cm (1–8in), and they develop from eggs picked up by mouth. They are common in puppies, who are frequently infected from the teats of the mother. If not eradicated, roundworms can obstruct the intestines, damage the gut wall and cause malnutrition in the puppies. The lungs may also be damaged and respiratory troubles ensue. Fortunately, roundworms are easily and safely eliminated by the use of a worming agent containing Piperazine, such as Coopane, which is obtainable from the vet and can be given as early as three weeks of age. If worms are passed, it is advisable to repeat the dose after two weeks, and again before the puppies leave for their new homes.

Tapeworms

These are common in adult dogs, especially in those fed on a diet of raw sheep tripe or infested with fleas, which may act as the intermediate host. Country dogs exercised in fields where sheep have grazed may also become infected. Fleas, sheep, cattle, deer, rabbits and hares all act as secondary hosts to various species of tapeworm, and can pass on the eggs to the dog.

The tapeworm grows from its scolex (head end), which becomes embedded in the wall of the intestine, anchored by hooks and suckers. Strings of flat, white segments develop from the scolex, and the whole worm may be a metre or more in length. The end segments, which are bags of eggs, become detached and are passed out with the dog's motions, where they appear as flat, white structures, about a centimetre long, which can be seen to move. In bad cases of infestation, dried segments can usually be seen attached to the hair round the anus.

In dosing for tapeworm, it is essential that the whole worm, especially the embedded scolex, is eliminated. If the scolex remains, another chain of segments soon develops from it, and no good will have been done. It is most important to obtain a good wormer from a vet and give the correct dose.

Fleas

The dog flea is larger than the human variety, dark brown in colour and rarely bites mankind. Fleas are most commonly found in the area of the back in front of the tail, over the loins, and in the head region. They breed in bedding, floor coverings, and accumulations of dirt in kennels and sleeping quarters. The best precaution against them is scrupulous cleanliness and careful incineration of used bedding material. A mildly infested dog may be treated with one of the various proprietary flea products on the market but, for serious cases, bathing with an insecticidal shampoo will probably be necessary. Kennels and floor coverings must also be treated.

Lice

Dogs can acquire lice if barley straw is used for bedding. Lice are commonly found in the vicinity of the ears and on the neck and legs. Unlike fleas, they breed on the body of the dog, and their eggs, known as nits, remain attached to the hair. They cause intense irritation, so any scratching, especially in young puppies, who are extra susceptible, should be investigated carefully. Adult lice can be killed with powders and insecticidal shampoos, but

Tell and Monarque, George Earl.

Earl of MacDona's two champions, Tell and Monarque, in a snowdrift came up for sale at Christies in 1991, but was withdrawn when bidding reached £7500. In the same year Christies sold for £2300 a fine large painting *St Bernard on the Edge of a Wood* by German artist Heinrich Sperling (1844–1924).

Twentieth century artists who have successfully painted the breed include F T Dawes, W Luker Jr, Norah Drummond and Arthur Wardle. The last of these, whose work is much sought after by collectors, died in 1948 at the age of 85. He is said to have produced 250 dog paintings for reproduction on Wills and Players cigarette cards, among them a fine head study of a St Bernard.

St Bernard on the Edge of a Wood, Heinrich Sperling.

Advertising agents

The fame and reputation of the breed has always been commercially exploited to advertise a variety of products, ranging from insurance to alcoholic drinks. One early insurance poster showed a St Bernard rescuing a small girl from the harbour at Marseille, and was issued on behalf of Zurich, a company based in Paris and offering cover against 'Les accidents et la Responsibilité Civile'.

Spratts issued a series of postcards of

champion dogs advertising their 'Patent Dog Cakes and Foods – Best for all Breeds'. In 1905, their St Bernard card featured a painting of Ch Hermione by the artist F T Dawes and recommended that the breed should be fed on 'Spratt's Fibrine Cakes, by Royal Warrant to HM The King'. In the same year, the book publishers Cassells & Co used a painting by Lilian Cheviot to advertise their *New Book of the Dog*. It featured Ch The Viking, who was a top winner at that time.

An advertisement for Zurich insurance showing a St Bernard rescuing a little girl.

St Bernards have always featured prominently in advertisements for food and drink, both human and canine. *To School Well Fed on Grape Nuts* was lithographed on a tin in 1917, and a Smooth dog carrying a large canister was used on a poster to champion the merits of Borwicks Baking Powder. In 1920, several St Bernard posters were issued by The Corvina Citrus Association, Los Angeles, to advertise 'Corvina Oranges – St Bernard Brand'. One of Jack and Eve Cooper's St Bernards was the model for the dog featured on cans of Pedigree Petfood. On the Continent, St Bernards are widely used to advertise chocolate. The Suchard Company use the breed to publicise their Milka brand, manufactured in Paris and Strasbourg.

When Sir Edwin Landseer painted a St Bernard with a barrel of brandy attached to its neck he started a connection between the breed and the hard stuff that has persisted to this day. As early as 1910 the breed was used in Schlitz beer advertisements, and in the same year it was featured in posters for Martell Brandy. Today, the makers of Hennessy Brandy still retain their connection with the breed, although they no longer present the brass-bound barrels, bearing their name, to top winners. Two of Mr E Millar's dogs were shown visiting

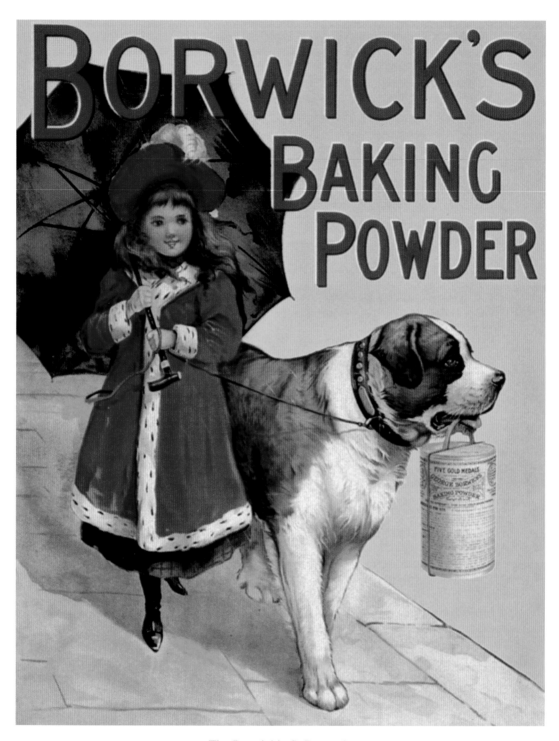

The Borwick's St Bernard.

the opera in a campaign on Hennessy's behalf in 1977.

Cigarette firms published numerous series of dog cards. Two of the best advertisements featuring St Bernards were the Player's card showing a head study painted by Arthur Wardle, and the larger De Reszke card showing a Saint puppy guarding a pair of gloves.

Charity collectors

The appeal of St Bernards to the public and the great size that makes their presence impossible to ignore mean that there are few breeds more successful as collectors for charity.

Saints have collected thousands of pounds on behalf of the St Bernard Trust (Registered Charity No. 328193), which was set up to cope with the problem of unwanted St Bernards (see

CHOCOLAT CACAO
SUCHARD

The Milka advertisement.

A Player's cigarette card, with head study.

Chapter 12). They have stood with their owners outside supermarkets, cinemas, garden centres and other places of business, often wearing brandy barrels converted to collecting boxes, or harnesses containing receptacles for contributions. The recent series of American films about the St Bernard Beethoven have provided a unique opportunity to appeal to lovers of the breed.

Other good causes have not been forgotten. Saints in Hastings have supported the RAF Wings Appeal, and a bitch in Scotland

Milkmen in the Berne area

who pulls a cart has raised large sums of money for the Canine Defence League and the Scottish Society for the Prevention of Cruelty to Children. These are just isolated examples of the good work done by St Bernards on behalf of charitable organisations.

Draught animals

At one time large dogs were frequently used on the Continent to pull small delivery carts, often loaded with milk. In Belgium in particular, draught dogs were fairly common. In Switzerland also, as the picture shows, St Bernards sometimes carried out this task, with assistance from their owners. They were also sometimes trained to haul sledges.

On the stage

When the great Plinlimmon was exported to America to appear in stage shows, a tradition was established which has persisted to this day. J M Barrie, who owned a St Bernard, introduced the caring dog Nana into the cast of *Peter Pan*. Barrie once wrote of his dog staring at him *through the red haws that make his eyes so mournful*. What else could this be but a Saint?

St Bernards are always great 'hits' when they appear on stage, and appear to relish all the applause and attention. This was obviously the case when Maureen Gwilliam's great bitch, Ch Mountside Movie Star, joined the cast of Gigi at a theatre in Newcastle. Two Saints bred by Miss Connie Clark behaved impeccably when taking part in a village pantomime in Sussex.

St Bernards have made many appearances in film and television. The classic comedy series *Father Dear Father* featured one of Mr and Mrs Attwood's Saints, Bernabella Christcon St Patsy. A St Bernard had a starring role in the screen production *Genevieve*. More recently one has rescued James Bond on film and appeared briefly in the BBC classic *Middlemarch*. And who can forget 'Beethoven'? The list is endless...

PAT dogs

Under the Pets As Therapy (PAT) scheme in this country, dogs are taken into hospitals and homes for the elderly to visit the sick and infirm, many of whom get comfort and enjoyment from their presence. Candidates for acceptance as PAT dogs must demonstrate high standards of docility and obedience. St Bernards are very popular members of PAT schemes. Mrs Carol Newton and her three St Bernards visit elderly patients at hospitals in Bolton.

Visiting the opera on behalf of Hennessy Cognac (captured picture from television).

A St Bernard in another rôle. Barnahely Byron (Green Star),
the mascot of the 58th Battalion of the Irish Army.

Appendix A

Champion	Sex	DOB	Sire	Dam	Breeder	Owner	CCs
1946							
Yew Tree St Christopher	d	14.9.43	Yew Tree St Bruno	Yew Tree St Filumena	Mrs C E Walker	A K Gaunt	3
1948							
St Christopher	d	31.5.44	Clearbrook St John	Modern Miss	E W Dovey	E Chasty	5
Caesario of Clairvaux	d	14.7.44	Freizland Lion	St Cecilia of Clairvaux	Miss E Watts	Breeder	3
Cornagarth Wendy of Flossmere	b	8.9.42	Jupiter of Priorsleigh	Prudence of Priorsleigh	T Lightfoot	A K Gaunt	6
Clearbrook Sally	b	13.9.44	Clearbrook St John	My Lady Jane	Miss L A Laidlaw	Miss I L Gross	4
Mountains Gypsy Girl	b	26.2.46	Copleydene Lucky Flight	Lady of the Mountains	Mr & Mrs E Farragher	Mrs A E Irving	5
1949							
Cornagarth Mountains Tiger	d	20.7.44	Copleydene Lucky Flight	Zena of the Mountains	Mr & Mrs E Farragher	A K Gaunt	4
Yew Tree St Errol of Priorsleigh	d	28.3.44	Yew Tree St Bruno	Yew Tree St Filumena	Mrs C E Walker	Mrs N Cox	3
Molino St Brittania	b	6.3.45	Ch Yew Tree St Christopher	Yew Tree St Anne	Dr E Heard	A K Gaunt	3
Lady St Maidell	b	10.1.46	Copleydene Lucky Flight	Alpine Lady	Miss J Walkden	Breeder	3
Snowbound Traveller's Joy of St Olam	d	21.9.44	St Marcus	Lady of Trees	Mr Wilder	W D Joslin	3
1950							
Snowbound Beau Cherie of St Olam	b	23.9.48	Ch Snowbound Traveller's Joy of St Olam	Snowbound Lassie	Mrs D C Wilder	W D Joslin	8
Cornagarth Comborrow St Ernesto	d	18.10.49	Ch Yew Tree St Christopher	Ch Lady St Maidell	Miss J Walkden	A K Gaunt	3
Cornagarth Bulldrummond of St Bury	d	2.10.46	St Marcuson	Copleydene St Lionetta	W F Barazetti	A K Gaunt	3
Thornebarton Bruno	d	23.9.46	Robin of Priorsleigh	Yew Tree St Gloria	Mrs C E Walker	Mrs G M Slazenger	3
Mountains Glamour Girl	b	16.4.45	Copleydene Lucky	Zena of the Mountains	Mr & Mrs E Farragher	Mrs E Graydon Bradley	7
1951							
Moorgate Violet	b	5.9.44	Beldene Barco	Moorgate May	W Barton	A J Gaunt	3
Boystown Cavalier	d	25.6.45	Robin of Priorsleigh	Yew Tree St Beatrice	Mrs N Cox	Mrs E Graydon Bradley	5
St Dominic of Brenchley	d	7.8.47	St Jude of Brenchley	Abbess of Brenchley	J B Knock	Mrs R L Walker	3
Cornagarth Culzean Nero	d	27.12.49	Ch Yew Tree St Christopher	Beldene Josephine	Mrs R M Bryce	A K Gaunt	3
Cornagarth Colonel	d	18.6.47	Ch Yew Tree St Christopher	Cornagarth Sandra	A K Gaunt	W A Jeffery & H Wilkinson	3

Champion	Sex	DOB	Sire	Dam	Breeder	Owner	CCs
St Olam Regent Prince	d	2.11.49	St Marcuson	Cynthia of St Olam	W D Joslin	Breeder	4
Cornagarth Cornbarrow St Oliver	d	18.10.48	Ch Yew Tree St Christopher	Ch Lady St Maidell	Miss J Walkden	A K Gaunt	3
Cornagarth Brenda	b	13.7.47	Cornagarth Gulliver	Cornagarth Georgia	A K Gaunt	Mrs A Rees	3
Melody of Priorsleigh	b	30.6.46	Robin of Priorsleigh	Yew Tree St Beatrice	Mrs N Cox	Breeder	3
Cornagarth Betty	b	13.7.47	Cornagarth Gulliver	Cornagarth Georgia	A K Gaunt	Breeder	
1952							
Brenda of Peldartor	b	16.7.49	Ch St Dominic of Brenchley	Cornagarth Belinda	Mrs R L Walker	Breeder	3
Beldene Portia	b	27.12.48	Daphnydene Bruno of Beldene	Daphnydene Annabella	Mrs J F Briggs	A K Gaunt	3
Mairead Masterpiece	d	27.12.49	Ch Yew Tree St Christopher	Beldene Josephine	Miss R M Bryce	Breeder	5
Cornagarth Marshall v Zwing Uri	d	7.4.47	Hasso v Zwing Uri	Christel v Moosberg	C Sigrist	A K Gaunt	4
1953							
Cornagarth Guardsman	d	5.4.51	Ch Cornagarth Marshall v Zwing Uri	Ch Cornagarth Cornborrow St Catherine	A K Gaunt	Breeder	5
Carol of Peldartor	b	6.1.50	Beldene Mikado	Cornagarth Dawn	Mrs R L Walker	Breeder	3
Cornagarth Cornborrow St Catherine	b	18.10.48	Ch Yew Tree St Christopher	Ch Lady St Maidell	Miss J Walkden	A K Gaunt	3
St Olam Sultan	d	15.8.51	Ch St Olam Regent Prince	Zena of St Olam	W D Joslin	Breeder	4
Colussus of Peldartor	d	6.1.50	Beldene Mikado	Cornagarth Dawn	Mrs R L Walker	Breeder	3
Cornagarth McNab	d	27.12.49	Ch Yew Tree St Christopher	Beldene Josephine	Mrs M Bryce	Mrs M Whiteley	5
1954							
Peldartor Anka v d Ducke Schlense	b	22.12.48	Conny v d Eilshorst	Undine v Hammoverland	Otto Harder	Mrs R L Walker	3
Terwin Caliph	d	8.5.49	Ch Yew Tree St Christopher	Ch Lady St Maidell	Miss J Walkden	A K Gaunt	3
Margurita of Normadene	b	7.8.51	Ch Cornagarth Marshall v Zwing Uri	Cornagarth Heatherbelle	Mrs M Whiteley	Mrs M Whiteley & N Davies	6
Cornagarth Monberno Anthony	d	4.1.51	Beldene Ajax	Monberno Belle	Rev M Brasil	A K Gaunt	3
1955							
What a Girl	b	24.4.52	The Ace of Mountsonia	St Winifred	Mrs L Townley	Breeder	3
Mairead Indian Prince	d	27.12.49	Ch Yew Tree St Christopher	Beldene Josephine	Miss R M Bryce	Breeder	3
Peldartor Lydia	b	1.11.52	Ch Colossus of Peldartor	Ch Brenda of Peldartor	Mrs R L Walker	Breeder	3

Champion	Sex	DOB	Sire	Dam	Breeder	Owner	CCs
Monberno Duke	d	4.1.51	Beldene Ajax	Monberno Belle	Rev M Brasil	Mrs O A Lees	4
Cornagarth Christopher	d	4.10.51	Ch Cornagarth Colonel	Ch Cornagarth Betty	A K Gaunt	Breeder	3
1956							
Brownie of St Bury	b	4.10.51	Ch Yew Tree St Christopher	Angelica of St Bury	W Barazetti	Breeder	3
Snowbound Cynthia	b	3.4.51	Snowbound Avalanche Lionheart	Joy of Snowbound Lassie	Mrs D Wilder	Miss R M Bryce	3
Peldartor Lucia	b	1.11.52	Ch Colossus of Peldartor	Ch Brenda of Peldartor	Mrs R L Walker	Breeder	3
Cornagarth Limelight	d	10.4.53	Ch Cornagarth Culzean Nero	Cornagarth My Own	J Quigley	A K Gaunt	3
Cornagarth Crysella	b	4.10.51	Ch Cornagarth Colonel	Ch Cornagarth Betty	A K Gaunt	Breeder	3
Peldartor Charnwood Bruno	d	15.1.52	Beldene Ajax	Monberno Belle	Rev M Brasil	Mrs R L Walker	3
St Olam Beauty	b	15.9.53	St Olam Mischa	St Olam Reedcourt St Babette	W D Joslin	Breeder	3
Peldartor Orrangit	d	4.1.54	Ch Peldartor Charnwood Bruno	Ch Carol of Peldartor	Mrs R L Walker	Breeder	3
Mairead Angus McNab	d	17.9.54	Ch Mairead Masterpiece	Ch Snowbound Cynthis	Miss R M Bryce	Breeder	6
1957							
Christcon St Anthony	d	21.5.54	Ch Cornagarth Culzean Nero	Cornagarth Comet	Mrs C Hutchings	Breeder	12
Peldartor Ranee	b	13.6.55	Ch Peldartor Charnwood Bruno	Ch Peldartor Anka v d Schlense	Mrs R L Walker	Breeder	5
Cornagarth Durrowabbey St Teresa	b	1.6.54	Ch Cornagarth Cornborrow St Oliver	Ch Cornagarth Thornebarton Jungfrau	Mrs G Slazenger	A K Gaunt	3
Cornagarth Thornebarton Jungfrau	b	20.9.51	Ch Cornagarth Marshall	Daphnydene Maxine	Mrs G Slazenger	A K Gaunt	3
Cornagarth Durrowabbey St Maria	b	1.6.54	Ch Cornagarth Cornborrow St Oliver	Ch Cornagarth Thornebarton Jungfrau	Mrs G Slazenger	A K Gaunt	4
1958							
Peldartor Rosseau	d	13.6.55	Ch Peldartor Charnwood Bruno	Ch Peldartor Anka v d Schlense	Mrs R L Walker	Breeder	3
Bernmont Felicity	b	21.5.54	Cornagarth Recorder of Bernmont	Bernmont Abbess	Mrs E Muggleton	J Harpham	3
Christcon St Arline	b	21.5.54	Ch Cornagarth Culzean Nero	Cornagarth Comet	Mrs C Hutchings	Breeder	3
Cornagarth Harvest of Durrowabbey	b	8.8.56	Castor v Ringelli	Ch Cornagarth Durrowabbey St Teresa	A K Gaunt	Breeder	3

Champion	Sex	DOB	Sire	Dam	Breeder	Owner	CCs
Cornagarth Just Right	d	25.9.56	Ch Cornagarth Limelight	Cornagarth Netta	Mrs A A Newton	A K Gaunt	3
Cornagarth Falco	d	23.6.54	Ch Cornagarth Guardsman	Ch Cornagarth Crysella	A K Gaunt	Breeder	3
1959							
Cornagarth Brittainia of Durrowabbey	b	31.5.57	Ch Cornagarth Guardsman	Ch Cornagarth Durrowabbey St Teresa	A K Gaunt	Breeder	3
Cornagarth Beverley of Durrowabbey	b	31.5.57	Ch Cornagarth Guardsman	Ch Cornagarth Durrowabbey St Teresa	A K Gaunt	Breeder	3
Prima Donna of Burtonswood	b	9.9.55	Ch Peldartor Charnwood Bruno	Cornagarth Coronet	Miss M Hindes	Breeder	3
Cornagarth Monbardon Sir Marcus	d	15.2.57	Cornagarth Durrowabbey St Patrick	Cornagarth Horsa	Mrs R M Clemerson	A K Gaunt	4
Christcon St Iris	b	18.2.57	Cornagarth Durrowabbey St Patrick	Cornagarth Comet	Mrs C Hutchings	Breeder	10
Cornagarth Birthday Boy of Durrowabbey	d	11.3.58	Cornagarth Benedict of Solentvale	Ch Cornagarth Durrowabbey St Teresa	A K Gaunt	Breeder	3
1960							
Cornagarth Defender of Durrowabbey	d	10.6.58	Ch Cornagarth Falco	Ch Cornagarth Durrowabbey St Maria	A K Gaunt	Breeder	3
Cornagarth Vanetta	b	14.2.56	Ch Cornagarth Christopher	Cornagarth Tosca	A K Gaunt	Breeder	3
Cornagarth Delilah of Durrowabbey	b	10.6.58	Ch Cornagarth Falco	Ch Cornagarth Durrowabbey St Maria	A K Gaunt	Breeder	3
Cornagarth Monbardon Sir Jonathan	d	15.2.57	Cornagarth Durrowabbey St Patrick	Cornagarth Horsa	Mrs R M Clemerson	Mrs C Bradley	3
Garry of Bryneithin	d	10.8.54	Bryneithin Masterpiece	Bryneithin Sandra of Normandene	Mrs S Lawton	Dr U Westell	4
Cornagarth Pied Piper	d	3.4.57	Cornagarth Durrowabbey St Patrick	Cornagarth Crystal	B Cherry	H Allen	5
1961							
Cornagarth Swiss Duchess	b	21.3.56	Ch Cornagarth Culzean Culzean Nero	Cornagarth Swiss Charmer	A K Gaunt	Breeder	3
Juno of Gresham	b	18.9.58	Ch Cornagarth Just Right	Cornagarth Veronica	Mrs B Dew	Mrs G M Allen	5
Cornagarth Burtonswood Easter Hero	d	31.3.58	Ch Cornagarth Just Right	Ch Prima Donna of Burtonswood	Miss M Hindes	A K Gaunt	3
Christcon St Jeremy	d	24.2.57	Christcon St Barco	St Colliers Genevieve	Mrs D Harrison	Mrs C Hutchings	4

Champion	Sex	DOB	Sire	Dam	Breeder	Owner	CCs
1962							
Cornagarth Keep On	d	7.11.59	Ch Cornagarth Defender of Durrowabbey	Ch Prima Donna of Burtonswood	Miss M Hindes	A K Gaunt	3
Cornagarth Master of Durrowabbey	d	10.5.59	Ch Peldartor Rosseau	Ch Cornagarth Durrowabbey St Maria	A K Gaunt	Breeder	3
Peldartor Cornagarth Nicholas	d	11.3.58	Cornagarth Benedict of Solentvale	Ch Cornagarth Durrowabbey St Teresa	A K Gaunt	Mrs R L Walker	3
Burtonswood Katrina	b	7.11.59	Ch Cornagarth Defender of Durrowabbey	Ch Prima Donna of Burtonswood	Miss M Hindes	Breeder	3
Cornagarth Excellence	d	15.1.61	Ch Cornagarth Defender of Durrowabbey	Cornagarth Robina	A K Gaunt	Breeder	3
Cornagarth Moira	b	19.2.60	Ch Cornagarth Monbardon Sir Marcus	Peldartor Wydello	Mrs A N Groves	A K Gaunt	4
1963							
Cornagarth Marina	b	19.2.60	Ch Cornagarth Monbardon Sir Marcus	Peldartor Wydello	Mrs A N Groves	A K Gaunt	3
Burtonswood Christcon St Olga	b	26.8.58	Ch Christcon St Jeremy	Christcon St Diana	Mrs C Hutchings	Miss M Hindes	4
Cornagarth Sensation	d	22.4.59	Ch Cornagarth Monbardon Sir Marcus	Cornarth Berna	H Tideswell	A K Gaunt	3
Peldartor Xcellence	d	20.9.58	Peldartor Jacques	Peldartor Ritchell	Mrs R L Walker	Breeder	4
1964							
Fernebrandon Agrippa	d	28.6.61	Ch Christcon St Jeremy	Fernebrandon Brita v Salmegg	Mrs Dixon	Dr U Westell	3
Cornagarth Romaine of Durrowabbey	b	29.10.61	Ch Cornagarth Keep On	Ch Cornagarth Delilah of Durrowabbey	A K Gaunt	Breeder	3
Cornagarth Democrat	d	10.6.58	Ch Cornagarth Falco	Ch Cornagarth Durrowabbey St Maria	A K Gaunt	Breeder	3
Cornagarth Minty of Maurbry	b	10.9.61	Ch Cornagarth Monbardon Sir Marcus	Burtonswood Easter Sue	Miss M Hindes	Mrs M Chapman	4
Cornagarth for Tops	d	4.2.62	Ch Cornagarth Monbardon Sir Marcus	Cornagarth Keep Me	A K Gaunt	Breeder	5
St Damian of Dale End	d	1.1.59	Ch Cornagarth Just Right	St Elizabeth of Dale End	Mr & Mrs F Read Pearson	Breeders	3
Cornagarth to Treasure of Brondeg	b	4.2.62	Ch Cornagarth Monbardon Sir Marcus	Cornagarth Keep Me	A K Gaunt	Breeder	4

Champion	Sex	DOB	Sire	Dam	Breeder	Owner	CCs
Peldartor Cornagarth Maracus	d	19.2.60	Ch Cornagarth Monbardon Sir Marcus	Peldartor Wydello	Mrs A N Groves	Mrs R L Walker	3
1965							
Fernebrandon Achilles	d	28.6.61	Ch Christcon St Jeremy	Fernebrandon Brita v Salmegg	Mrs Dixon	Dr J Holmes	3
Helga of Gresham	b	15.10.58	Ch Cornagarth Monbardon Sir Marcus	Gilda of Gresham	Mrs Dew	Breeder	3
Cornagarth Adam	d	30.5.62	Ch Cornagarth Burtonswood Easter Hero	Christcon St Nadia	A K Gaunt	Breeder	3
Peldartor Ireton	d	20.4.61	Ch Peldartor Cornagarth Nicholas	Ch Peldartor Ranee	Mrs R L Walker	Breeder	3
Peldartor Julich	b	14.11.61	Ch Peldartor Cornagarth Nicholas	Ch Peldartor Ranee	Mrs R L Walker	Breeder	3
Cornagarth Koon	d	30.12.62	Ch Cornagarth Keep On	Cornagarth Debutant	Mrs M Hall	A K Gaunt	3
Cornagarth Cortina	b	3.3.63	Ch Cornagarth Keep On	Ch Cornagarth Delilah of Durrowabbey	A K Gaunt	Dr & Miss Leonard	3
Snowranger Arcadian	d	31.10.62	Ch Cornagarth Keep On	Snowranger Lucky Charm	Mrs C Bradley & P Hill	B Driver	3
Cornagarth Truthful	b	7.3.63	Ch Cornagarth Master of Durrowabbey	Ch Cornagarth Moira	A K Gaunt	Breeder	3
1966							
Cornagarth Robin of Durrowabbey	d	29.10.61	Ch Cornagarth Keep On	Ch Cornagarth Delilah of Durrowabbey	A K Gaunt	Breeder	3
Cornagarth Wanda	b	5.1.63	Cornagarth Memory of Durrowabbey	Cornagarth Elsa	A K Gaunt	Breeder	3
Peldartor Reubens	d	30.12.63	Ch Peldartor Xcellence	Ch Peldartor Julich	Mrs R L Walker	Breeder	3
Cornagarth True Love	b	7.3.63	Ch Cornagarth Master of Durrowabbey	Ch Cornagarth Moira	A K Gaunt	Miss M Hindes	3
Broxhead Cornagarth Annabelle	b	17.8.61	Ch Cornagarth Birthday Boy of Durrowabbey	Ch Cornagarth Moira	A K Gaunt	Miss M Hindes	3
Cornagarth Demon	d	13.1.64	Ch Cornagarth Democrat	Broxhead Cornagarth Sun Tan	Miss M Hindes	A K Gaunt	3
Panbride Lady Freda	b	24.8.62	Ch Christcon St Jeremy	Claypottis Lady Aurora	Miss J Fyffe	Breeder	3
1967							
Snowranger Chloris	b	22.12.63	Snowranger Tello v Saulient	Snowranger Saucy Sue	Mrs C Bradley	Mrs C Bradley & P Hill	3
Kelvaston Sir Christopher	d	24.12.64	Ch Cornagarth Sensation	Burtonswood Veronique	Dr & Miss Leonard	Breeders	3

Champion	Sex	DOB	Sire	Dam	Breeder	Owner	CCs
Cornagarth Burtonswood	b	11.12.64	Ch Cornagarth For Tops	Ch Cornagarth True Love	Miss M Hindes	A K Gaunt	3
Cornagarth To Be	d	4.2.62	Ch Cornagarth Monbardon Sir Marcus	Cornagarth Keep Me	A K Gaunt	L/Col Sir T Cook	4
Burtonswood Brown Velvet	b	6.7.65	Ch Cornagarth For Tops	Burtonswood Easter Sue	Miss M Hindes	Breeder	3
Cornagarth Cordo	d	27.11.65	Ch Cornagarth For Tops	Cornagarth Suzette	Dr Chesterfield	A K Gaunt	3
Peldartor Abbott	d	6.6.65	Ch Peldartor Xcellence	Peldartor Accra	Mrs R L Walker	Breeder	3
Bernmont Yana	b	2.2.63	Ch Christcon St Jeremy	Cornagarth Sophia	Mrs I Oliver	Mrs & Miss Muggleton	3
1968							
Cornagarth Stroller	d	27.10.66	Ch Cornagarth Adam	Ch Cornagarth Burtonswood Princess	A K Gaunt	Breeder	4
Cornagarth Mickado	d	16.12.63	Ch Cornagarth Birthday Boy of Durrowabbey	Cornagarth Elsa	A K Gaunt	Breeder	3
Bernmont Warlord	d	10.11.64	Bernmont Snowranger Statesman	Bernmont Carol	Mrs & Miss Muggleton	Breeders	8
Burtonswood Cornagarth Molly	b	20.6.66	Ch Cornagarth For Tops	Cornagarth Melanie	A K Gaunt	Miss M Hindes	3
Cornagarth Burtonswood Bonanza	d	26.7.66	Ch Cornagarth Keep On	Burtonswood Bitter Sweet	Miss M Hindes	A K Gaunt	3
1969							
Sennowe Riga	b	24.11.64	Ch Cornagarth To Be	Cornagarth Katrina	L/Col Sir T Cook	Breeder	3
Burtonswood Bright Star	b	11.6.67	Ch Cornagarth Adam	Burtonswood Bitter Sweet	Miss M Hindes	Breeder	6
Cornagarth Carlos	d	8.9.67	Ch Cornagarth Cordo	Cornagarth Carol	A K Gaunt	Breeder	3
Burtonswood Beloved	b	13.5.68	Ch Cornagarth Cordo	Burtonswood Bitter Sweet	Miss M Hindes	Breeder	5
Bernmont Victoria	b	1.10.64	Bernmont Christcon St Rajah	Bernmont Teresa	Mrs & Miss Muggleton	Breeders	3
1970							
Snowranger Bas v d Vrouwenpolder	d	26.5.66	Hektor v Liebiwil	Helga v Hutwil	A Schrama	Mrs C Bradley & P Hill	3
Cornagarth Kelvaston Bo-Peep	b	31.7.65	Ch Cornagarth For Tops	Burtonswood Veronique	Dr & Miss Leonard	A K Gaunt	3
Cornagarth He's Grand	d	18.6.68	Ch Cornagarth Robin of Durrowabbey	Ch Cornagarth Burtonswood Princess	A K Gaunt	Breeder	3
Burtonswood Black Diamond	d	11.1.69	Ch Cornagarth Stroller	Burtonswood Be Wonderful	Miss M Hindes	Breeder	6

Champion	Sex	DOB	Sire	Dam	Breeder	Owner	CCs
1971							
Burtonswood Big Time	b	6.2.68	Cornagarth Luck	Ch Cornagarth True Love	Miss M Hindes	M J Braysher	3
Peldartor Zigismund	d	30.11.65	Ch Peldartor Xcellence	Ch Peldartor Julich	Mrs R L Walker	Breeder	3
Cornagarth Marquisite	b	14.8.67	Ch Cornagarth Koon	Cornagarth Cordette	A K Gaunt	Mrs M Gwilliam	3
Burtonswood Black Perle	b	11.1.69	Ch Cornagarth Stroller	Burtonswood Be Wonderful	Miss M Hindes	Breeder	3
Cornagarth Shanta	b	27.10.66	Ch Cornagarth Adam	Ch Cornagarth Burtonswood Princess	A K Gaunt	Breeder	4
Cornagarth Mirabelle	b	4.8.67	Ch Cornagarth Koon	Cornagarth Cordette	A K Gaunt	M J Braysher	3
Cornagarth Luke	d	13.12.65	Ch Cornagarth For Tops	Ch Cornagarth Romaine of Durrowabbey	A K Gaunt	Mr J & Miss P Hill	3
Ghyllendale Aristocrat	b	16.11.69	Cornagarth Luck	Ghyllendale Cornagarth Juliana	Mr & Mrs B Everall	Breeders	3
1972							
Burtonswood Be Bright	b	15.6.70	Ch Cornagarth Stroller	Ch Burtonswood Beloved	Miss M Hindes	Breeder	4
Cornagarth Fleur	b	7.1.69	Ch Cornagarth Stroller	Cornagarth Cordette	A K Gaunt	Breeder	3
Daphnydene Karro v Birkenkopf	d	21.4.69	Alex v Pava	Gundi v Birkenkopf	O Ulrich	Mrs D Ackybourne	3
Lindenhall High Commissioner	d	11.4.71	Cornagarth Kuno v Birkenkopf	Cornagarth Adelaide	Mr & Mrs R J Beaver	Breeders	15
Burtonswood Bethney	b	12.6.69	Ch Cornagarth Stroller	Ch Burtonswood Cornagarth Molly	Miss M Hindes	Breeder	3
Bernmont Gilda	b	8.8.69	Bernmont Iceberg	Cornagarth Michaela	Mrs M Harris	Mrs & Miss Muggleton	4
Burtonswood Be Mine	b	15.6.70	Ch Cornagarth Stroller	Ch Burtonswood Beloved	Miss M Hindes	Breeder	3
Cornagarth Burtonswood Be Great	d	15.6.70	Ch Cornagarth Stroller	Ch Burtonswood Beloved	Miss M Hindes	A K Gaunt	3
1973							
Burtonswood Bossy Boots	d	10.7.71	Cornagarth Kuno v Birkenkopf	Ch Burtonswood Beloved	Miss M Hindes	Breeder	13
Cornagarth Heiki of Pittforth	b	20.3.71	Cornagarth Kuno v Birkenkopf	Cornagarth Burtonswood Becoming	A K Gaunt	Mr & Mrs M Whitelaw	10
Burtonswood Black Tarquin	d	16.12.70	Cornagarth Kuno v Birkenkopf	Ch Burtonswood Black Perle	Miss M Hindes	A K Gaunt & Miss M Hindes	13
Bernmont Griselda	b	8.8.69	Bernmont Iceberg	Cornagarth Michaela	Mrs M Harris	Mrs & Miss Muggleton	3
Panbride Sir Warran of Pittforth	d	4.8.68	Westernisles Fernebrandon Brutus	Panbride Lady Magnolia	Miss Milne	Mr & Mrs M Whitelaw	3

Champion	Sex	DOB	Sire	Dam	Breeder	Owner	CCs
Burtonswood Bossy Bess	b	10.7.71	Cornagarth Kuno v Birkenkopf	Ch Burtonswood Beloved	Miss M Hindes	Breeder	4
1974							
Lindenhall Highlight	b	11.4.71	Cornagarth Kuno v Birkenkop	Cornagarth Adelaide	Mr & Mrs R J Beaver	Breeders	5
Burtonswood Be Able	b	15.6.70	Ch Cornagarth Stroller	Ch Burtonswood Beloved	Miss M Hindes	Mr & Mrs B Loftus	4
Pittforth Angus	d	21.1.73	Ch Cornagarth Burtonswood Be Great	Ch Cornagarth Heiki of Pittforth	Mr & Mrs M Whitelaw	Breeders	4
Snowranger Cascade	d	6.1.71	Snowranger Cornagarth Lucky	Snowranger Dresden	Mrs C Bradley & P Hill	Miss J McMurray	7
Lindenhall High & Mighty	b	11.4.71	Cornagarth Kuno v Birkenkopf	Cornagarth Adelaide	Mr & Mrs R J Beaver	Breeders	4
1975							
Lindenhall High Hopes	b	8.6.70	Ch Cornagarth Carlos	Anna Lisa of Thalberg	Mr & Mrs R J Beaver	Breeders	3
Lindenhall High Commander	d	11.4.71	Cornagarth Kuno v Birkenkopf	Cornagarth Adelaide	Mr & Mrs R J Beaver	Breeders	3
Lindenhall Calamity Jane	b	3.11.73	Ghyllendale Harvester	Ch Lindenhall High & Mighty	Mr & Mrs R J Beaver	Mrs E Ridley	11
Lindenhall Capability Brown	d	3.11.73	Ghyllendale Harvester	Ch Lindenhall High & Mighty	Mr & Mrs R J Beaver	Breeders	7
Cornagarth Cara	b	27.8.72	Cornagarth Kuno v Birkenkopf	Cornagarth Phoebe	A K Gaunt	Mrs G Topping	3
1976							
Burtonswood Black Lace	b	2.8.73	Ch Burtonswood Bossy Boots	Ch Burtonswood Black Perle	Miss M Hindes	Breeder	3
Burtonswood Be True	d	28.7.74	Ch Burtonswood Bossy Boots	Cornagarth Chiquita	Miss M Hindes	Mrs M K Humphrey	3
Whaplode Desdemona	b	9.9.73	Cornagarth Kuno v Birkenkopf	Cornagarth Alma	Mr & Mrs J Harpham	Breeders	5
Whaplode Eros of Bernmont	d	16.2.74	Cornagarth Askan	Cornagarth Anna	Mr & Mrs J Harpham	Mrs & Miss Muggleton	4
Lindenhall High Ball	d	6.9.72	Ch Lindenhall High Commissioner	Lindenhall Sweet Charity	Mr & Mrs R J Beaver	Breeders	3

Champion	Sex	DOB	Sire	Dam	Breeder	Owner	CCs
1977							
Coatham Star Shine	b	13.11.73	Ch Burtonswood Black Tarquin	Northern Star of Coatham	Mr & Mrs G Gwilliam	Breeders	10
Alpentire Paters Princess	b	16.6.74	Ch Cornagarth Burtonswood Be Great	Alpentire Snowranger Forest Charm	Mrs J McMurray	Breeder	8
Benem Lady Guinevere	b	9.10.74	Lucky Strike of Cornagarth	My Lady Emma	Mr & Mrs R Miller	Mr & Mrs M Wensley	5
Whaplode King	d	25.10.75	Whaplode Emporer	Burtonswood Black Jewel	Mr & Mrs J Harpham	Breeders	3
Lindenhall High Admiral	d	11.4.74	Cornagarth Kuno v Birkenkopf	Cornagarth Adelaide	Mr & Mrs R J Beaver	Mrs D Campbell	3
Gerunda Buster	d	13.8.75	Prad King of Gerunda	Snowranger Lindsey	Messrs & Mrs James	Breeders	3
Cornagarth Dominant Dominic of Bermmont	d	21.10.74	Ch Burtonswood Black Tarquin	Braypass Audrey	A K Gaunt	Mrs & Miss Muggleton	4
1978							
Lindenhall Fast & Furious	b	3.4.74	Ch Lindenhall High Commissioner	Ch Lindenhall High Hopes	Mr & Mrs R J Beaver	Breeders	3
Burtonswood Be Fine	b	28.7.74	Ch Burtonswood Bossy Boots	Cornagarth Chiquita	Miss M Hindes	Mrs G Topping	6
Burtonswood Be Fire	d	28.7.74	Ch Burtonswood Bossy Boots	Cornagarth Chiquita	Miss M Hindes	Mrs J Burr	3
Pittforth Calum	d	6.12.75	Ch Panbride Sir Warran of Pittforth	Ch Cornagarth Heiki of Pittforth	Mr & Mrs M Whitelaw	Breeders	3
Whaplode Ivanhoe	d	27.3.75	Whaplode Emporer	Ch Whaplode Desdemona	Mr & Mrs J Harpham	Breeders	4
Coatham Commissioner's Aide	d	23.3.75	Ch Lindenhall High Commissioner	Northern Star of Coatham	Mr & Mrs G Gwilliam	Mrs H Taylor	3
Braypass Sportsman	d	28.9.76	Ch Burtonswood Bossy Boots	Braypass Butchers Girl	M J Braysher	Breeder	5
Burtonswood Barensa	b	4.1.74	Cornagarth Tough Nut	Ch Burtonswood Bossy Bess	Miss M Hindes	S Oates	4
Grand Duke of Lindenhall	d	26.3.76	Ch Lindenhall Capability Brown	Hardacre Wotagem	Mrs A Stepto	R J Beaver & Miss W Machin	3
1979							
Whaplode Margaret	b	28.5.76	Ch Whaplode Ivanhoe	Whaplode Amy	Mr & Mrs J Harpham	Breeders	3
Topvalley Wogan's Winner	d	4.1.78	Ch Burtonswood Bossy Boots	Lena of Cornagarth	Mrs G Topping	Breeder	19
Pittforth Catriona	b	6.1.75	Ch Panbride Sir Warran of Pittforth	Ch Cornagarth Heiki of Pittforth	Mr & Mrs M Whitelaw	Breeders	4

Champion	Sex	DOB	Sire	Dam	Breeder	Owner	CCs
Sandcroft Saroscha	b	7.6.76	Ch Burtonswood Black Tarquin	Burtonswood Benera	A J Osman	Breeder	6
Lindenhall Sarah Siddons	b	4.9.75	Ch Lindenhall Capability Brown	Ch Lindenhall Fast & Furious	Mr & Mrs R J Beaver	Breeders	5
Topvalley Chardas	d	1.7.77	Ch Burtonswood Bossy Boots	Burtonswood Black Secret	Mrs G Topping	E N Davies	3
Fairydales Demon King	d	30.7.76	Ch Burtonswood Be Fire	Wildmere Natalia	Mrs J Burr	E J Atkins	3
1980							
Roddinghead Agent Kris of Knockespoch	b	4.1.79	Alpentire Commission Agent	Roddinghead Prudence	A Stevens	Mrs S Roberts	10
Swindridge Catherine	b	10.3.77	King v St Klara Kloster	Swindridge Madam Annaliese	Mr & Mrs M Wensley	Breeders	4
Burtonswood Be Friendly	d	27.4.77	Ch Burtonswood Bossy Boots	Burtonswood Be Lovely	Miss M Hindes	Mr & Mrs Scrivens	5
Swindridge Madam Danielle	b	9.8.77	Ch Burtonswood Bossy Boots	Swindridge Madam Acacia	Mr & Mrs M Wensley	Breeders	3
Whaplode Unique	d	2.6.78	Ch Whaplode Ivanhoe	Whaplode Juliette	Mr & Mrs J Harpham	Breeders	22
Bernmont Nola	b	1.4.76	Ch Whaplode Eros of Bernmont	Benem Lady Constance of Bernmont	Mrs & Miss Muggleton	Breeders	3
Topvalley Joanne	b	2.10.79	Topvalley Just Jamie	Topvalley Anna	Mrs G Topping	Breeder	7
1981							
Alpentire on Commission	d	8.2.77	Ch Lindenhall High Commissioner	Alpentire Paters Promise	Mrs J McMurray	G Gwilliam	3
Burtonswood Black Duke	d	13.3.76	Ch Burtonswood Bossy Boots	Burtonswood Black Brocade	Miss M Hindes	Mrs S Boulden	3
Maurbry Mini Sota of Bernmont	b	30.3.77	Heidan Easter Greetings	Benem Lady Be Good	Mrs M Chapman	Mrs & Miss Muggleton	4
Swindridge Sir Dorian	d	9.8.77	Ch Burtonswood Bossy Boots	Swindridge Madam Acacia	Mr & Mrs M Wensley	Breeders	5
Bernmont Aristocrat	d	29.9.78	Ch Cornagarth Dominant Dominic of Bernmont	Bernmont Odessa	Mrs & Miss Muggleton	Breeders	3
Be Elect of Burtonswood	b	18.8.77	Ch Burtonswood Bossy Boots	Braypass Olga	M J Braysher	Mr & Mrs G Gwilliam	4
Benem Sir Galahad	d	9.10.74	Lucky Strike of Cornagarth	My Lady Emma	Mrs R Miller	Mrs J Evans	8
Be Glad of Burtonswood	d	24.8.77	Ch Burtonswood Bossy Boots	Burtonswood Balrina	Mrs & Miss Cockings	E G Lloyd	4

Champion	Sex	DOB	Sire	Dam	Breeder	Owner	CCs
Topvalley Anna	b	16.1.76	Ch Burtonswood Bossy Boots	Toppos Delight	Mrs G Topping	Breeder	3
1982							
Burtonswood Be Mighty	d	29.8.79	Tweedle Dee of Burtonswood	Topvalley Carasel of Burtonswood	Miss M Hindes	Breeder	4
Braypass Boomerang	b	26.8.79	Ch Topvalley Wogans Winner	Braypass Special	M J Braysher	Breeder	3
Bernmont Alexandra	b	29.9.78	Ch Cornagarth Dominant Dominic of Bernmont	Bernmont Odessa	Mrs & Miss Muggleton	Breeders	3
Irrissa of Bernmont	b	12.1.80	Whaplode Julian of Bernmont	Pittforth Dallas	Mr & Mrs M Whitelaw	Mrs & Miss Muggleton	3
Swindridge Ferdinand	d	2.1.78	Ch Swindridge Sir Dorian	Swindridge Catherine	Mr & Mrs M Wensley	Breeders	4
Pittforth Fleur	b	15.1.80	Whaplode Julian of Bernmont	Pittforth Cassandra	Mr & Mrs M Whitelaw	Breeders	5
Morning Star of Hartleapwell	b	7.2.80	Ch Benem Sir Galahad	Icelandic Maiden of Hartleapwell	Mrs J McMurray	Mrs J Evans	4
Ravensbank Hardtime	b	7.12.77	Ch Whaplode Ivanhoe	Whaplode Lucille	Mrs P Stammers	Breeder	5
Maurbry Modelman	d	18.2.80	Ch Topvalley Wogans Winner	Benem Lady Be Good	Mrs M Chapman	Breeder	3
1983							
Lucky Charm of Whaplode	b	10.4.81	Ch Whaplode Unique	Ch Roddinghead Agent Kris of Knockespoch	Mr & Mrs J Harpham	Breeders	24
Lady Prudence of Middlepark	b	5.11.77	Ch Benem Sir Galahad	Middlepark Harriet	Walker	Mrs S Boulden	4
Burtonswood Be Favourite	d	27.4.77	Ch Burtonswood Bossy Boots	Burtonswood Be Lovely	Miss M Hindes	Breeder	3
Whaplode My Lord	d	25.4.81	Ch Whaplode Ivanhoe	Whaplode Juliette	Mr & Mrs J Harpham	Breeders	17
Bernmont Charlotte	b	21.6.79	Whaplode Julian of Bernmont	Bernmont Rhona	Mrs & Miss Muggleton	Breeders	4
Swindridge Madam Hazel	b	6.5.80	Swindridge Sir Edward	Swindridge Madam Acacia	Mr & Mrs M Wensley	Breeders	3
Bavush Drina	b	2.5.79	Whaplode Tobias	Fairydales Folly	Mrs T Ridings	Breeder	5
1984							
Laird O'Glayva of Treeburn	d	23.9.79	Alpentire Commission Agent	Icelandic Maiden of Hartleapwell	Miss C Hennan	Mr & Mrs R Gardner	5
Knockespoch Berenice	b	10.4.81	Ch Whaplode Unique	Ch Roddinghead Agent Kris of Knockespoch	Mrs S Roberts	Breeder	5
Maurbry Message	d	4.10.80	Ch Whaplode Unique	Benem Lady Be Good	Mrs M Chapman	Breeder	3

Champion	Sex	DOB	Sire	Dam	Breeder	Owner	CCs
Mountain Hunter of Vallefrey	d	13.12.81	Ch Whaplode Unique	Snowrambler of Adelja	Miss J Peters	Mr & Mrs G Craven	7
Topvalley Karl	d	10.9.80	Ch Topvalley Wogans Winner	Topvalley Carrin Withasea	Mrs G Topping	Breeder	11
Swindridge Madalene	b	1.4.82	Ch Swindridge Ferdinand	Swindridge Geraldine	Mr & Mrs M Wensley	Breeders	3
Schnozzer Huggy Bear	d	23.7.83	Topvalley JR	Olympic Princess	Mr & Mrs P Girling	Breeders	11
Braypass Marina	b	20.5.81	Ch Cornagarth Dominant Dominic of Bernmont	Braypass Special	M J Braysher	Breeder	3
Bernadino Maxi	b	21.10.83	Ch Topvalley Wogans Winner	Ravensbank Katy Cube of Bernadino	Mr & Mrs Lux	Breeders	9
1985							
Merridale Bouncer	d	8.6.81	Topvalley Heidis Boy	Bavush Daydreamer	Clarke	Miss E Cooper	6
Swindridge Laura	b	6.5.81	Ch Swindridge Ferdinand	Swindridge Geraldine	Mr & Mrs M Wensley	Mr & Mrs P Girling	5
Knockespoch Highline	b	2.5.83	Knockespoch Boy	Fastacre Royale Empress of Knockespoch	Mrs S Roberts	Mr, Mrs & Miss Bateman	4
Footloose Freddy	d	4.6.81	Maurbry Marzipan	Maurbry Bethany	Miss G Burrell	Mrs S Thorpe	4
Coatham Hermes	b	1.8.82	Ch Whaplode Unique	Coatham Ides of March	Mr & Mrs G Gwilliam	Breeders	5
Swindridge Mathew	d	1.4.82	Ch Swindridge Ferdinand	Swindridge Geraldine	Mr & Mrs M Wensley	Breeders	5
Finetime Sardonyx	d	11.11.83	Whaplode My Major	Fastacre Spartan Diamond	Mr & Mrs Findlay	Miss Thomas & Mr Churchill	4
Maurbry Maisy Maiden	b	25.3.81	Ch Whaplode Unique	Maurbry My Maiden	Mrs M Chapman	Mrs A L Barnes	3
1986							
Pankraz v d Drei Helman of Bernmont	d	8.10.82	Casar v Holdersberg	Herma v d Drei Helman	Mahrlein & Schreiber	Miss P Muggleton	3
Bernadino Winterberg	d	21.10.83	Ch Topvalley Wogans Winner	Ravensbank Katy Cube of Bernadino	Mr & Mrs Lux	Breeders	5
Hartleapwell Secret Love	b	6.1.84	Ch Maurbry Message	Ch Morning Star of Hartleapwell	Mrs J Evans	Breeder	11
Coatham Gin N Tonic	b	1.2.83	Coatham Rum N Black	Ch Be Elect of Burtonswood	Mr & Mrs G Gwilliam	Mr & Mrs D Owen	3
Marlender Moonraker	d	21.12.79	Ch Lindenhall Capability Brown	Kempshott Tia Maria	Mr & Mrs R Martin	Breeders	3
Hartleapwell Magic Moments	b	6.1.84	Ch Maurbry Message	Ch Morning Star of Hartleapwell	Mrs J Evans	Breeder	5
Middlepark Grand Monarque	d	16.12.83	Middlepark Dark Knight	Middlepark Bridgette	Mrs S Boulden	Breeder	5

Champion	Sex	DOB	Sire	Dam	Breeder	Owner	CCs
Woodruff Felicity	b	12.7.82	Ch Topvalley Karl	Woodruff Bush Baby	Mr & Mrs Harrison	B Markham	5
Bernadino Fedor	d	21.10.83	Ch Topvalley Wogans Winner	Ravensbank Katy Cube of Bernadino	Mr & Mrs Lux	Breeders	6
Finetime the Great Bear	d	17.4.84	Arambaskh Statesman	Pilgrimwood Gorgeous Girl	Mr & Mrs Findlay	Miss Thomas & Mr Churchill	12
Treeburn Challenger	d	26.10.84	Ch Laird O'Glayva of Treeburn	Penvalla of Treeburn	Mr & Mrs R Gardner	Breeders	7
1987							
Coppice Bertie	d	1.10.84	Ch Marlender Moonraker	Ch Maurbry Maisy Maiden	Mrs A Barnes	Breeder	13
Bavush Natasha	b	5.12.82	Bavush Mr Smoothy	Lady Genevieve of Bavush	Mrs T Ridings	Breeder	4
Denbow Miss Muffit	b	16.5.85	Gruline North Wind	Ch Coatham Gin N Tonic	Mr & Mrs Owen	Breeders	10
Finetime Amethyst of Bermont	b	11.11.83	Whaplode My Major	Fastacre Spartan Diamond	Mr & Mrs Findlay	Mrs Sobolewski	8
Swindridge Rochester	d	8.8.84	Ch Pankraz v d Drei Helman of Bermmont	Ch Swindridge Madalene	Mr & Mrs M Wensley	Breeders	3
Swindridge Geraldine	b	28.9.79	Swindridge Sir Edward	Swindridge Catherine	Mr & Mrs M Wensley	Breeders	3
1988							
Earl of Alvaston	d	21.5.86	Ch Finetime the Great Bear	Bavush Amy	J Taylor	Breeder	5
Montaryie Galestorm	d	20.7.85	Montaryie Exclusive Edit	Zekeyta Bonnie Bess	Mrs Maxwell	Mr & Mrs Long Doyle	3
My Lucky Lady	b	21.5.86	Ch Finetime the Great Bear	Bavush Amy	J Taylor	Breeder	8
Finetime Sputnik	b	17.4.84	Arambaskh Statesman	Pilgrimwood Gorgeous Girl	Miss Thomas & Mr Churchill	Breeders	7
Oatfield Nero	d	12.9.85	Ch Burtonswood Be Mighty Mighty	Demeroshea Sensation of Oatfield	S Oates	Miss M Hindes	3
Hartleapwell Must Be Magic	b	4.11.86	Ch Whaplode My Lord	Ch Hartleapwell Magic Moments	Mrs J Evans	Breeder	9
Bishopsway Moses of Whaplode	d	18.8.85	Ch Whaplode My Lord	Jatrose Wendy's Beauty	Mr & Mrs Cooke	Mr & Mrs J Harpham	12
Hartleapwell Stormy Magic	b	4.11.86	Ch Whaplode My Lord	Ch Hartleapwell Magic Moments	Mrs Evans	B Allen	6
Sooty Big Bad Wolf	d	15.1.85	Ace of Clubs	Blacklace Legacy	Mrs Yates	Mr & Mrs Brennan	3
1989							
Hartleapwell Midnite Magic	d	4.11.86	Ch Whaplode My Lord	Ch Hartleapwell Magic Moments	Mrs J Evans	Breeder	5

Champion	Sex	DOB	Sire	Dam	Breeder	Owner	CCs
Hartleapwell Touch of Magic	b	4.11.86	Ch Whaplode My Lord	Ch Hartleapwell Magic Moments	Mrs J Evans	Breeder	3
Bernies Tuesday Special	b	15.1.85	Ace of Clubs	Black Lace Legacy	Mrs P Yates	Breeder	3
Finetime Temptress	b	9.7.87	Ch Finetime the Great Bear	Inkerman Rogue of Finetime	Miss Thomas & Mr Churchill	R Bradley	4
Bernegardens JR of Fastacre (Swe Ch)	d	24.1.84	Int Ch Castlewoods Yamaha	Swe Ch Mars Dons Cotttonelle	B Halvorsen	Mr, Mrs & Miss Bateman	3
Bernmont Murdoch	d	31.1.86	Bernmont Diplomat	Petrava of Swindridge & Bernmont	Miss Muggleton	Breeder	3
Schnozzer Latest Edition	d	4.10.85	Ch Schnozzer Huggy Bear	Ch Swindridge Laura	Mr & Mrs Girling	Breeders	8
Saranbeck Sweep	b	3.6.86	Saranbeck Skymaster	Saranbeck So What	Mrs D Fawcett	Breeder	4
Winterbergs Boy	d	16.8.87	Ch Bernadino Winterberg	Zermatt Contessa	R Young	Mrs J Lux	17
Lynbern Dennis The Menace of Meadowmead	d	18.9.87	Ravensbank Simply Solomen at Sileeda	Finetime Solar System	Mrs Winn	Mr & Mrs R Byles	39
1990							
Coatham Suffragette	b	30.6.87	Coatham Ripe Harvest	Coatham Andromeda	Mr & Mrs G Gwilliam	Breeders	4
Meadowmead Juliana	b	13.7.88	Ch Montaryie Galestorm	Coatham Mary Rose	Mr & Mrs R Byles	Breeders	9
Swindridge Andrea	b	5.9.87	Ch Bernmont Murdoch	Swindridge Quanda	Mr & Mrs M Wensley	Breeders	5
Dragonville Lord Snooty at Coatham	d	17.6.87	Coatham Ripe Harvest	Saranbeck Splash	Mrs Frost	Mr & Mr G Gwilliam	4
Mountside Mauritania of Meadowmead	b	21.8.87	Ravensbank Simply Solomen at Sileeda	Coatham Britania	Mr & Mrs Stokell	Mr & Mrs R Byles	6
Schnozzer Dark Golden	b	4.10.85	Ch Schnozzer Huggy Bear	Ch Swindridge Laura	Mr & Mrs Girling	Breeders	3
Finetime Celtic Princess	b	9.7.87	Ch Finetime the Great Bear	Inkerman Rogue at Finetime	Miss Thomas & Mr Churchill	Breeders	4
Mountside Movie Star	b	15.10.88	Ch Finetime the Great Bear	Coatham Britania	Mr & Mrs Stokell	Mr & Mrs G Gwilliam	22
Ballincollig of Barnahely	d	21.12.85	Ir Ch Glasslyn Malachite	Beauty's Dream	Mrs G Barry	Breeder	3
Ballingeary of Barnahely	d	21.12.85	Ir Ch Glasslyn Malachite	Beauty's Dream	Mrs G Barry	Breeder	3
1991							
Fastacre High Society	b	24.5.87	Pankraz v d Drei Helmen of Bernmont	Ch Knockespoch Highline	Mr, Mrs & Miss Bateman	Breeders	3
Finetime Saxon Alchemist	d	9.7.87	Ch Finetime the Great Bear	Inkerman Rogue of Finetime	Miss Thomas & Mr Churchill	Breeders	3
Bernadino Fedor's Boy	d	24.11.89	Ch Bernadino Fedor	Bernadino Marie Therese	Mrs J Lux	Breeder	4
Nor Ch Bernegardens Buckpasser	d	20.3.88	Bernegardens Rigoletto	Nor Ch Dein Hards Zinnia	Ms Halvorsen	Mrs N Goodwin	8

Champion	Sex	DOB	Sire	Dam	Breeder	Owner	CCs
Kenine Catrian of Bernadino	b	2.4.89	Amblair Dekaha Anni	Ravensbank Up Town Girl	Mr & Miss Sheen	Mrs J Lux	8
Mountside Serenade at Culrain	b	30.9.88	Ch Earl of Alvaston	Mountside Moonshine	Mr & Mrs Stokell	Mrs MacLaughlan 3	
Broadheath Executive Class	b	15.4.89	Ch Schnozzer Latest Edition	Fitza Bootie	Mr & Mrs Gooch	Breeders	3
1992							
Saranbeck Sayra at Marlender	b	2.4.90	Swindridge Columbus	Ch Saranbeck Sweep	Mrs D Fawcett	Mrs L Martin	13
Grimoire Banshee	b	23.4.90	Gerunda Napoleon at Leontonix	Bernmont Helga	Mr & Mrs Edwards	Breeders	5
Swindridge Cassius	d	12.1.88	Ch Bernmont Murdoch	Ch Swindridge Madalene	Mr & Mrs M Wensley	Breeders	3
Mountside Starlight at Alpentire	b	25.8.90	Finetime Brother Gabriel	Ch Mountside Movie Star	Mr & Mrs Stokell	Mrs J McMurray	9
Oringlow Hudson	d	19.1.91	Oringlow Freewheeler	Czyantie Kiss an Tell of Oringlow	Mr & Mrs P Swindlehurst	Breeders	4
1993							
Bavush Wallis of Offenbach	b	25.9.89	Offenbach High Plains Hero	Swindridge Trina	Mrs T Ridings	J Taylor	3
Offenbach Field Marshall	d	4.4.90	Offenbach High Plains Hero	Offenbach Florence	J Taylor	Breeder	5
Whaplode Be Our William	d	23.2.91	Ch Schnozzer Latest Edition	Whaplode Be Illustrious	Mr & Mrs Harpham & Mrs M Pearl	Breeders	36
Bavush Classic Lady	b	20.10.91	Ch Swindridge Columbus	Bavush Who's Dodgy Dodgy	Mrs T Ridings	Mrs L Martin	8
Holdgrange Majician	d	15.6.91	Ch Bernmont Murdoch	Swindridge Penelope	Mrs Grainger	Mr & Mrs Walton	5
Schatzberger Brandysnap	b	3.9.89	Swindridge Columbus	Schatzberger Amathyst	Mr & Mrs M Chapman	Mr Chapman & Mrs Bannister	3
Coatham Good News For Wyandra	d	16.1.90	Ch Schnozzer Latest Edition	Ch Coatham Suffragette	Mr & Mrs G Gwilliam	Miss Swaine-Williams	7
1994							
Meadowmead Empress Queen	b	11.10.91	Ch Lynbern Dennis The Menace of Meadowmead	Meadowmead Santa Barbara	Mr & Mrs R Byles	Breeders	7
Saranbeck Smugglers Gold	b	2.12.92	Ch Coatham Good News for Wyandra	Saranbeck Shamrock	Mrs D Fawcett	Breeder	8
Timeside Mr Sloba-Doba	d	13.7.91	Finetime Sir Brock	Ch Mountside Solitaire	Mr & Mrs Davis	Breeders	17

Champion	Sex	DOB	Sire	Dam	Breeder	Owner	CCs
Abbotsbury Impression	d	15.3.92	Ch Bernegardens Buckpasser	Abbotsbury Foolish Touch	Mr & Mrs Goodwin	Breeders	5
Middlepark Lettice	b	1.12.92	Ch Timeside Mr Sloba-Doba	Middlepark Gabriella	Mrs S Boulden	Breeder	12
Middlepark Meridian	d	1.12.92	Ch Timeside Mr Sloba-Doba	Middlepark Gabriella	Mrs S Boulden	Breeder	6
1995							
Meadowmead Helena	b	28.7.93	Ch Lynbern Dennis The Menace of Meadowmead	Meadowmead Santa Barbara	Mr & Mrs R Byles	Breeders	5
Whaplode Be Smart	b	1.1.92	Ch Bishopsway Moses of Whaplode	Whaplode My Wildfire	Mr & Mrs Harpham & Mrs M Pearl	Breeders	4
Mountside Secret of Campsie	b	25.8.90	Finetime Brother Gabriel	Ch Mountside Movie Star	Mr & Mrs Stokell	Mr & Mrs Simpson	4
1996							
Abbotsbury Ailanthus	d	8.5.94	Ch Abbotsbury Impression	Swindridge Wanda	Mr & Mrs Goodwin	Breeders	3
Middlepark Araminter	b	15.10.94	Ch Middlepark Meridian	Coatham The Campaigner of Middlepark	Mrs S Boulden	Breeder	4
Whaplode Beyond Pardon	b	15.5.91	Ch Schnozzer Latest Edition	Whaplode Be Lucky & Mrs Pearl	Mr & Mrs Harpham	Breeders	3
Mountside Solitaire	b	1.8.89	Ch Dragonville Lord Snooty at Coatham	Mountside Melody	Mr & Mrs Stokell	Mr & Mrs Davis	3
Whaplode Beyond Valour	d	7.11.93	Ch Whaplode Be Our William	Ch Whaplode Be Smart	Mr & Mrs Harpham & Mrs Pearl	Breeders	4
Ravensbank The Wizard	d	1/1/92	Finetime Fiun McCoole	Ravensbank Soly's Legacy	Mr & Mrs Stammers	Mr & Mrs I McLaughlan	3

Appendix B

Family Trees of Notable Male Champions

Male Champions in Direct Line from Berndene Prinz von Rigi

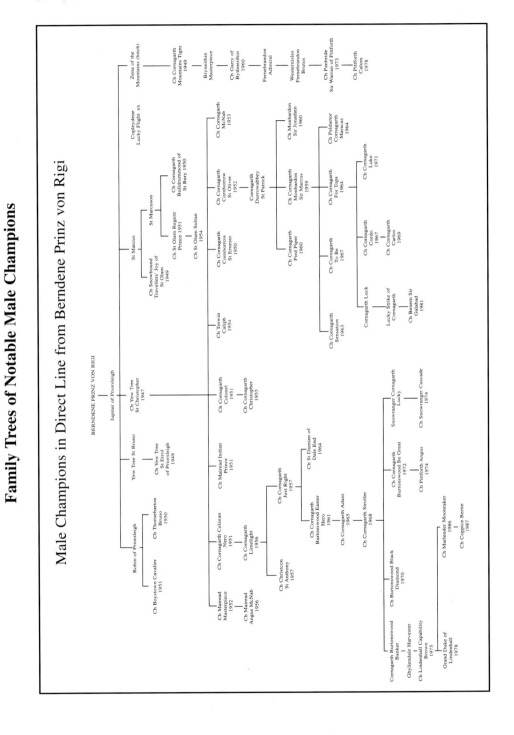

Male Champions in Direct Line from Fabius of Priorsleigh

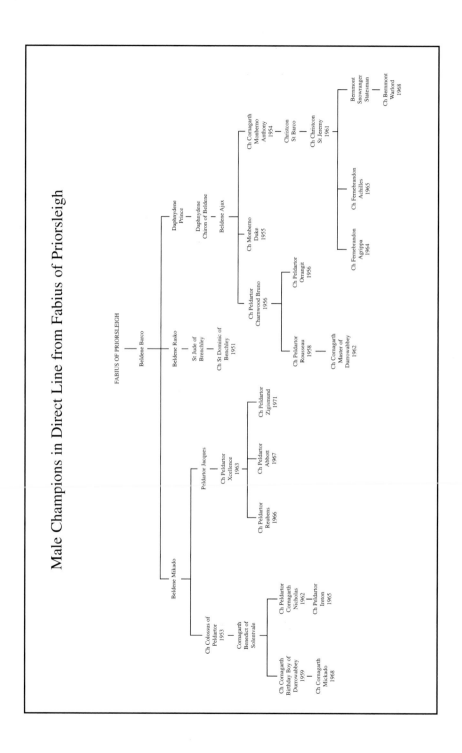

Family Trees of Notable Male Champions

Male Champions in Direct Line from Ch Cornagarth Marshall von Zwing Uri

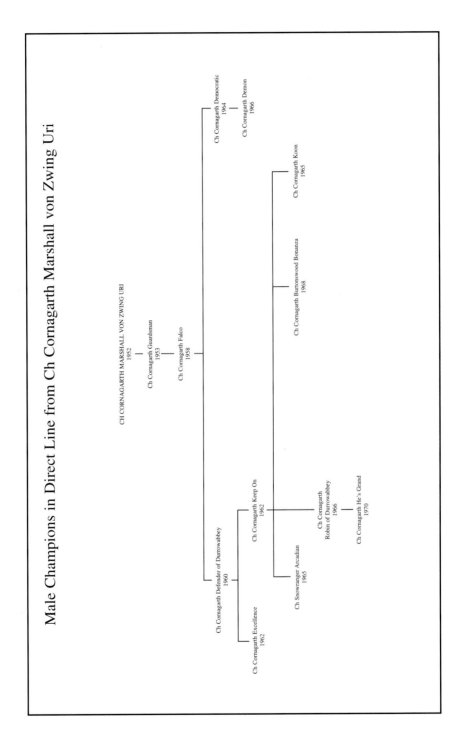

Male Champions in Direct Line from Alex von Pava

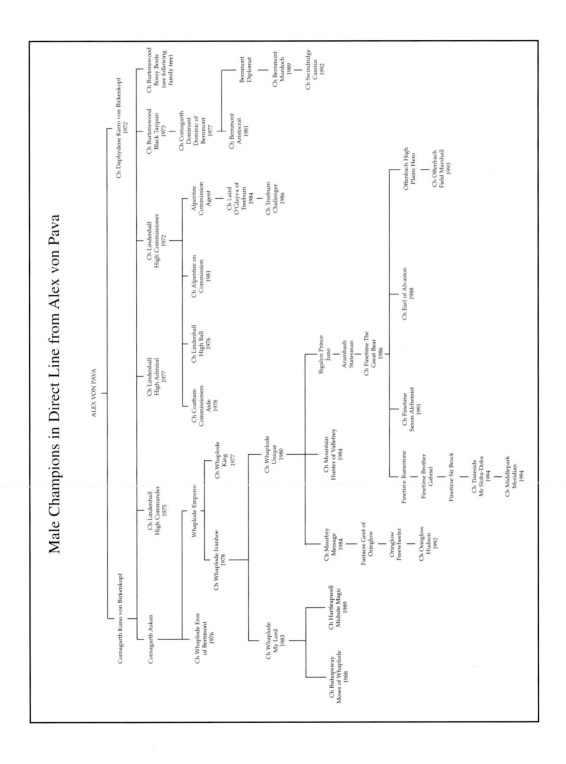

Family Trees of Notable Male Champions

Male Champions Direct in Line to Alex von Pava through Ch Burtonswood Bossy Boots

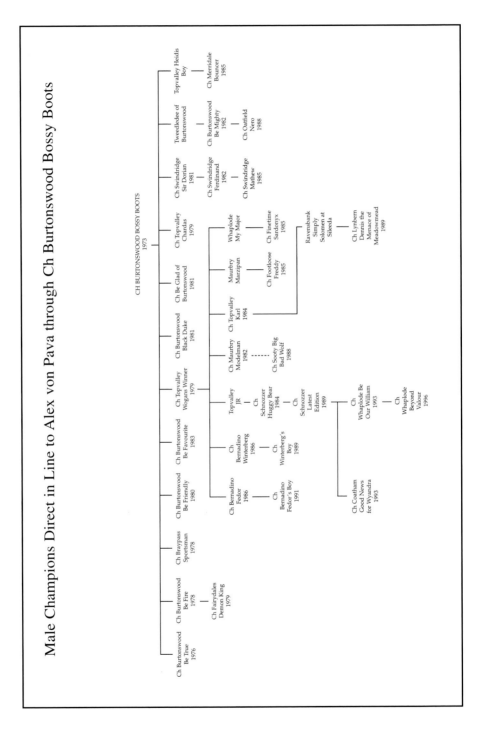

Useful Addresses

Great Britain

The Kennel Club
1–5 Clarges Street
Piccadilly
London
W1Y 8AB
Tel: 0171–493 6651

Since contact addresses for breed clubs change quite frequently, it is probably best to contact The Kennel Club for details of your nearest one. They are:

The Eastern St Bernard Club

The English St Bernard Club

The South of England St Bernard Club

The St Bernard Club of Scotland

The United St Bernard Club

Overseas

Fédération Cynologique Internationale
13 Place Albert I
B–6530
Thuin
BELGIUM
Tel: 071/59.12.38   Fax:071/59.22.29

Schweizerische Kynologische Gesellschaft
(The Swiss Kennel Club)
Langgastrasse 8
Postfach 8217
CH–3001
Bern
SWITZERLAND
Tel: 0041/313015819   Fax: 0041–31/302 02 15

This picture, taken in 1980, shows Richard, my husband, relaxing with some of our Lindenhall Saints. Richard held the Lindenhall affix jointly with me until he died after a long and brave struggle against cancer. It has not been easy to revise and update this book about the breed he loved without his encouragement, but I am sure he would have considered it a worthwhile task.
Photo: *Daily Mirror*

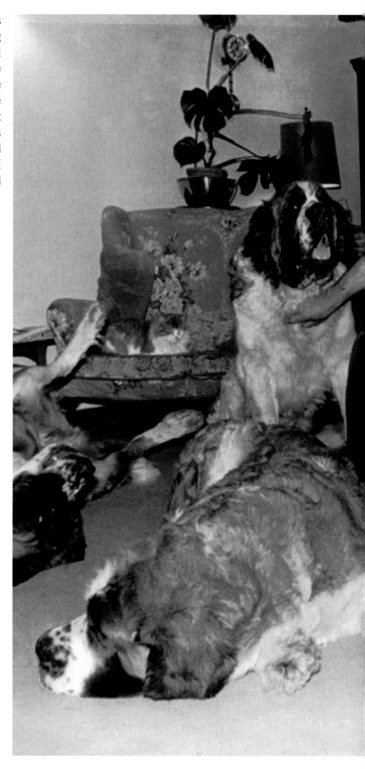

Index